HAPPINESS IS SOMETHING THAT HAPPENS.
CONTENTMENT IS SOMETHING WE CHOOSE.

FINDING
CONTENTMENT
IN A
DISAPPOINTING
WORLD

Fran —
I wish you God's richest
blessings — Love, Kathy

Kathy Collard Miller

Phil. 4:11

NAVPRESS ●®

A MINISTRY OF THE NAVIGATORS
P.O. BOX 6000, COLORADO SPRINGS, COLORADO 80934

The Navigators is an international Christian
organization. Jesus Christ gave His followers the
Great Commission to go and make disciples
(Matthew 28:19). The aim of The Navigators is
to help fulfill that commission by multiplying
laborers for Christ in every nation.

NavPress is the publishing ministry of The Navigators. NavPress publications are tools to help
Christians grow. Although publications alone
cannot make disciples or change lives, they can
help believers learn biblical discipleship, and
apply what they learn to their lives and
ministries.

Printed in the United States of America

Contents

To
the loving memory of
Bob Noble
whose contentment grew stronger
even when battling cancer.

Author

Kathy Collard Miller maintains a busy schedule as a writer and a speaker at women's seminars and retreats. She has written two books: *Out of Control* and *When Love Becomes Anger,* about how God delivered her from being an abusive mother.

Kathy has shared her exciting story on many Christian TV programs. She is a graduate of Florence Littauer's Advanced C.L.A.S.S. (Christian Leaders and Speakers Seminar).

Kathy and her husband, Larry, live in Placentia, California, with their two children.

Acknowledgments

My gratitude and love to the four special women of my writing critique group whose insightful suggestions have made me a better writer: Jennifer Botkin-Maher, Pattye Christensen, Beverly Hamilton, and Neva B. True.

I'd also like to thank my editor, Traci Mullins, whose wise editing improved this book.

And thank you, Richard Baltzell, for suggesting that I write a book on contentment.

1
The Quest for Contentment

Several years ago discontent was my middle name. I hated my life and thought I could never be content. The mother of a newborn and a two-year-old, I didn't like being "just" a mother. I looked around at my house and thought, "Why can't I be out evangelizing the world for You, Lord, instead of keeping house? Why do I have to be holed up with two kids who don't appreciate the godly influence I'm trying to give them? No matter how much I clean house or try to be the perfect mother and wife, no one appreciates it or cares. I want to do anything other than what I'm doing right now!"

I somehow sensed God wanted me to be content with the place where He'd put me, but that knowledge only made me feel condemned. I "should" have been content, but I wasn't. I "should" have been thanking God for the privilege of raising children, and for all the blessings He'd given me. But those "shoulds" only condemned me more because I wasn't at all thankful for the place where God had placed me.

I wanted everything to be different. I wanted to start Bible studies, not change the diapers of an infant. I wanted to converse with adults, not a two-year-old. I wanted to have a husband home on the weekends, not a husband who was gone working two jobs. I wanted to be like my friend who had it all together, not myself with my flaws and weaknesses.

If someone had offered me a one-way ticket away from my circumstances, I would have said, "I'll have my suitcase packed in thirty minutes!" Contentment with who I was or my circumstances was the last possible thing I thought I could achieve at that point in time.

Maybe you can relate to the way I felt. All of us have areas of our lives in which we're not content. We know we *should* be content, but somehow the shoulds don't change our dissatisfaction. In fact, the shoulds make our discontent deepen because they accentuate that God must be very unhappy with us. Why? Because we aren't being grateful for what He's given us. Yet instead of doing something about this, we continue to focus on what we don't have and what could be different, rather than on being grateful for what we do have.

This is the struggle of the discontented person. It was my struggle when I was that dissatisfied mother. Yet God worked in my life and brought me to a place of contentment. It was a beautiful process of growth that brought me out of the negative thinking of discontent into a luxurious contentment in the Lord that included thanking Him for who He made me to be and where He'd put me. It also included becoming grateful for a husband who didn't fulfill all my expectations and for circumstances that weren't my preference.

During that troubled time, I read about the apostle Paul's contentment and admired him. He wrote that he endured imprisonments, beatings, lashings, stonings, and shipwrecks. He was in danger from rivers, robbers, his own countrymen, the Gentiles, the city, the wilderness, the sea, false brethren, sleepless nights, hunger, thirst, cold, and exposure.

Paul concluded this list of trials by saying, "Most gladly, therefore, I will rather boast about my weaknesses, that the power of Christ may dwell in me. Therefore I am well content with weaknesses, with insults, with distresses, with persecutions, with difficulties, for Christ's sake; for when I am weak, then I am strong" (2 Corinthians 12:9-10). In another place Paul wrote, "Not that I speak from want; for I have learned to be content in whatever circumstances I am" (Philippians 4:11).

When I read all that Paul went through and realized that my troubles didn't compare to his, I wondered how I'd ever become content. I doubt that any of us have experienced what Paul experienced, yet if he could learn contentment, then I believe we can too. But it requires a process of growth.

The Lord took me through a process of growth into contentment over a period of time, and I believe He can do the same for you. My growth process into contentment is the basis for this book, but this book includes more than just my experience. You'll be reading about other people who have discovered God's touch of contentment amid difficult circumstances and trials—people who are content even though disease threatens their lives, other people disappoint them, unemployment robs them of possessions, and death steals their loved ones.

You might be experiencing these kinds of trauma. Or

maybe you just sense a need for greater contentment. You might be a mother at home with toddlers who seem to demand too much and rob you of contentment. Maybe your job stability is uncertain and you're convinced that contentment can't be a part of your life until you make that situation secure. Possibly, some person makes your life miserable and you tell yourself you'll be content when that person changes. Or you may be in great pain from some disease and can't even think straight, much less focus on contentment. There are any number of situations and circumstances that can rob us of contentment.

Stick with me while we go on a journey to discover how contentment can be a part of your life, if it's not already. You may find your skepticism melting away as you find out with me that we can embrace contentment for each of our lives. If it is a part of your life, let's make sure it stays there!

2
The Myths of Contentment

Maybe you're still not convinced that contentment is possible regardless of circumstances. Unfortunately, that is one of the myths that surround contentment. The myths include: contentment is only possible with perfect circumstances and perfect people; contentment is the same as positive thinking and happiness; and achieving contentment is a passive process in which we don't need to make any choices.

These myths color our perception and have a way of hampering our ability to actively build contentment into our lives. I was captive to these myths myself. I was convinced that I could only become content once my children and husband were perfect and somehow happiness enveloped my life. I also incorrectly believed that contentment wasn't something I choose, but something that would sweep over me when everything else was right in my life.

I had a lot to learn. The myths made me blind to God's viewpoint on contentment. It took time before He broke through my misguided perceptions and steered me into correct thinking. So with this second chapter, we'll be examining these myths and clearing the fog surrounding them. Then you'll be able to see more perceptively the truth about contentment.

But before we destroy these myths, let's discover what contentment really is. Normally we think of contentment as being so satisfied with what you have or what you are that you do not desire something more or different.

Joseph Addison said, "The utmost we can hope for in this world is contentment." Contentment amid whatever circumstances surround us truly is the ultimate. It means trusting God for every area of our lives, believing that He is the loving controller who doesn't allow anything to come into our lives except that which He has approved. Epictetus said, "I am always content with that which happens, for I think that which God chooses is better than what I choose."

But whatever perspective we reach about contentment can be clouded by the myths or counterfeits, so let's examine these now.

Myth #1—Contentment is a result of perfectionism.
Sometimes we have the attitude that "as soon as I become perfect, I'll finally be content." We keep striving for the perfection that will give us contentment amid our circumstances.

Yet, the truth is that none of us are going to be perfect in this lifetime. Therefore we must *learn* to be content, as Paul says, in the midst of what is happening around us. The hard times are the very opportunities when contentment in us will glorify the Lord the most.

This concept is clearly stated by Chuck Swindoll in his book *Standing Out*.

"Someday when the kids are grown, things are going to be a lot different. The garage won't be full of bikes, electric train tracks on plywood, sawhorses surrounded by chunks of two-by-fours, unfinished 'experimental projects,' and the rabbit cage.

"Someday when the kids are grown, the kitchen will be incredibly neat. The sink will stay free of sticky dishes, the garbage disposal won't get choked on rubber bands or paper cups, and we won't lose the tops to jelly jars, catsup bottles, the peanut butter, the margarine, or the mustard.

"Someday when the kids are grown, the instrument called a 'telephone' will actually be available. It won't look like it's growing from a teenager's ear.

"Someday when the kids are grown, I'll be able to see through the car windows. Fingerprints, tongue licks, sneaker footprints, and dog tracks (nobody knows how) will be conspicuous by their absence.

"Someday when the kids are grown, we will return to normal conversations. You know, just plain American talk. 'Gross' won't punctuate every sentence seven times.

"Yes, someday when the kids are grown, things are going to be a lot different. The house will be quiet . . . and calm . . . and always clean . . . and empty . . . and filled with memories . . . and lonely . . . and we won't like that at all. And we'll spend our time not looking forward to *Someday* but looking back to *Yesterday*. And thinking, 'Maybe we can baby-sit the grandkids and get some life back in this place for a change!'"[1]

The harried housewife thinks contentment will come when the kids can drive and she doesn't have to carpool. The disgruntled father searches for lost tools, and he figures he'll be content once the kids are out of the house. And each one of us thinks that as soon as life is perfect, we'll be content. Then we must remember: contentment is for right now, in the midst of the imperfect situations of our lives.

Myth #2—Contentment is just positive thinking.
Contentment *is* a matter of perspective, but it's more than positive thinking. Contentment doesn't bury its head in the sand and refuse to acknowledge the negative or unsatisfying things around us. No, contentment is a state of mind that recognizes the negative and unpleasant things in life, but chooses to focus on God.

Mary Slessor knew about contentment. A young single woman, at the turn of the century she left Scotland for a part of Africa infested with disease and indescribable danger. Once, after a particularly draining day, she found herself trying to sleep in a crude jungle hut. Of that night she wrote, "I am not very particular about my bed these days, but as I lay on a few dirty sticks laid across and covered with a litter of dirty corn-shells, with plenty of rats and insects, three women and an infant three days old alongside, and over a dozen sheep and goats and cows outside, you don't wonder that I slept little. But I had such a comfortable quiet night in my own heart."[2]

You can be sure that Mary's contentment wasn't the result of refusing to acknowledge she was surrounded by rats. No, she was very aware of all those things. Her contentment was the result of peace with God.

Most of us won't be called upon to choose contentment amid such difficult circumstances as Mary experienced. But whatever circumstances surround us, we'll be able to be content, not because we're ignoring the difficulty and just thinking "positively," but because we're at peace with God.

Myth #3—Contentment is the same as happiness.

Many people think they can never achieve contentment because they can't imagine being happy about certain difficult situations in their lives. There is hope for them because contentment is not the same as being happy.

Happiness is an emotion that results from pleasant circumstances. It's very "fickle" and can appear and disappear depending upon what's going on in our lives. It doesn't require any choice.

Contentment, on the other hand, is an inner trusting in God that may or may not be expressed with an outward happiness. Being content means believing that God is in control of the circumstances I've handed over to Him, regardless of how life appears.

But making that choice can be hard. My writer friend Neva B. True has shared with me how difficult it was for her to find contentment. She kept trying to find it by being happy. She says, "I tried to find contentment in many things: a job change for my husband, a move to a better house with coordinated furniture, an attractive wardrobe, and perfect kids. I thought finding those things would bring contentment into my life. Only through the Lord's grace has He convinced me that 'a tent or a cottage, why should I care; they're building a mansion for me over there.' Now I don't depend upon happiness for my contentment. I've learned that it comes from Jesus."

Neva has learned a valuable lesson. Contentment is different from happiness. Happiness is something that happens to you, but contentment is something we choose to have.

Myth #4—Contentment is passive.

As I'm walking beside the quiet waters of contentment, my first inclination is to think of it as passive, just accepting whatever circumstances come along. At first glance, contentment seems to rule out action, with no need to make decisions or set goals.

This, however, is a false picture. Being content doesn't eliminate the responsibility of making decisions and establishing goals. It means having a balance between relaxing in God's control and yet responding with active obedience.

I learned this principle on a recent Father's Day. I had been in a wonderful state of contentment for almost a year, but on this Father's Day, I grew discontented. I watched Larry lying on the couch all day watching TV and desperately wanted him to interact with the family. Darcy played with neighborhood friends, and I became frustrated when I tried to teach my son, Mark, to ride a bicycle.

I heard the neighbors playing and laughing in their pool and thought, "Now that's what I want on a Father's Day. A family playing together in a pool."

Discontent crept over me until tears stung my eyes. "Why can't things be different? Why can't our family be closer on Father's Day?" I wanted to scream. I was convinced I could no longer choose to be content because I didn't have the emotional energy.

I escaped to the bedroom, knelt by the bed, and poured out my discontent to the Lord. After I released my frustration, I slowly began to see that even though I didn't have the strength to choose to be content, the Lord could empower me as I made a choice to obey Him.

I prayed, "Lord, please empower me to trust You for all these dissatisfying circumstances. I give thanks for the progress that has been made in my marriage. I renew my commitment to trust You for the changes You want. Thank You. I love You. Amen."

I then decided to do what I could to choose contentment. I set the table with china and silver for a special dinner that would bring the family together for at least a short time. Busying myself with this act of love eventually caused my discontent to slip away.

That Father's Day was one of the many times God has used to continue to help me grow into contentment. Today, I am the most content I've ever been. I love life, yet could be discontented about many things and people if I didn't keep letting go of my own desires and welcoming God's plan as it unfolds. With God's help, I have determined to trust Him and accept whatever He has designed for my life. That doesn't mean I don't have goals, ambitions, and plans, but it does mean God's plan is more important than my plans.

We've learned that contentment can occur during imperfect circumstances, that it's more than just positive thinking, that it's not the same as happiness, and that it's not passive. With these myths exploded, we can continue on our journey. In the next chapter, we'll find out where contentment starts.

NOTES: 1. Charles R. Swindoll, *Standing Out* (Portland, Oreg.: Multnomah Press, copyright 1979 by Charles R. Swindoll, Inc.), pages 100-102, used by permission.
2. Gordon MacDonald, *Ordering Your Private World* (Nashville: Thomas Nelson, 1984), page 26, used by permission.

3
Where Contentment Starts

If contentment comes from trusting God and moving along according to His timetable, then we must first know God in order to experience that contentment. He has determined that there is a specific way through which He wants us to come to know Him. Jesus said, "I am the way, and the truth, and the life; no one comes to the Father, but through Me" (John 14:6). Jesus made it clear that the only way to know God is through Him. As we experience the assurance that God has accepted us as His children, contentment will result. Therefore, God's contentment *with* me begins the process of contentment *in* me.

Donna is a good example of this. Before she became a

Christian, she wasn't content with her life. She kept expecting the next planned event to satisfy her yearning for happiness. Yet, no matter how fun or satisfying the event would turn out to be, as soon as it was over, she still experienced the same longing and yearning for purpose and contentment.

Along with this craving, it seemed to her that time was playing tricks on her. Because she was never content with her circumstances and always looking ahead for something that would fulfill her, time slipped by faster and faster. As soon as she realized that the event didn't satisfy her, she would regret having been so miserable the previous few days. There was no way for her to regain that lost time. All she could think about was how she had wasted it. Then she began looking forward to the next potentially fulfilling situation or event.

After struggling through this cycle of frustration and lack of purpose, she visited her boyfriend's church. When the salvation message was given, she seemed to hear it clearly for the first time, even though she had grown up attending church. She prayed, asking Jesus to forgive her sins and take over her life. She claimed 2 Corinthians 5:17 that said she is a new creature. Over a period of time, as Bible study and prayer became more important to her, she knew she was indeed a new creature through God's working.

After several months, she remembered her former dissatisfaction when she looked for a fun time to fulfill her life. She realized those old gnawing, restless feelings had diminished. She certainly hadn't "arrived" at perfect contentment, but she knew she was growing in her ability to believe God's promises. Even when those old patterns of responding to life crept back, it became easier to recognize them. Overcoming them wasn't always instantaneous (and that could be discouraging at times), but at least she was making progress.

Maybe you're like Donna, continually seeking contentment through circumstances, events or people. Well, there's good and bad news. The bad news is that there can be no contentment without knowing God personally because only He fills the void in you that yearns for contentment and purpose. Even though becoming a Christian won't eliminate every feeling of discontent, it will give you the power to grow in contentment. The good news is that you can know God by inviting Jesus Christ into your life as your Savior and Lord.

Have you ever done that? I hope so. But if not, you can turn to Him right now and know that you've started a new life and are on your way to Heaven.

The first step is to realize that we are all sinners. No matter how righteous we feel, we still have sinned; we're all children of disobedience (Ephesians 2:2). Everyone is! "Yes, all have sinned; all fall short of God's glorious ideal" (Romans 3:23, TLB).

But the good news is that even though we have gone our own way, apart from God, He still loves us very, very much. You've most likely heard John 3:16 before, but have you ever put your name into it and made it your own personal verse? Try it now, with my paraphrase: "For God loved _____ (your name) so much that He gave His only Son to die on the Cross for _____ sins, so that if _____ believes in Him, _____ shall not perish but have eternal life."

Second, we must realize that sin will cause us to die eternally, as Romans 6:23 explains: "The wages of sin is death, but the free gift of God is eternal life through Jesus Christ our Lord" (TLB).

We can't do anything about our sin, but Jesus can. In fact, He's already taken care of it. Romans 5:8 says, "God showed his great love for us by sending Christ to die for us while we were still sinners" (TLB).

We can never be good enough to deserve eternal life, so instead, God offers it to us as a free gift. "Because of his kindness you have been saved through trusting Christ. And even trusting is not of yourselves; it too is a gift from God. Salvation is not a reward for the good we have done, so none of us can take any credit for it" (Ephesians 2:8-9, TLB).

Yet, just as a birthday gift is not yours until you unwrap it and take it for your own, this free gift of salvation is not yours until you accept it and believe that God has given it to you. The apostle John stated about Jesus, "To all who received him, he gave the right to become children of God. All they needed to do was to trust him to save them. All those who believe this are reborn!—not a physical rebirth resulting from human passion or plan—but from the will of God" (John 1:12-13, TLB).

If you desire to know Christ, pray something like this: "Heavenly Father, thank You for sending Jesus to die on the Cross for my sins. I realize I have lived apart from You, but now I want Jesus, through Your Holy Spirit, to come into my life, to cleanse me of my sin and take control of my life. From this point on, I give myself to You so that You can work Your plan in me. In Jesus' name. Amen."

You can be sure that Jesus came into your life when you asked Him, and He wants you to have that assurance. He promises to come into our lives, and He always keeps His promises. "So whoever has God's Son has life; whoever does not have his Son, does not have life. I have written this to you who believe in the Son of God so that you may *know* you have eternal life" (1 John 5:12-13, TLB, italics added).

The decision you made right now or in the past to receive Christ makes you justified before God. The concept of justification has a lot to do with helping us achieve contentment, and so we'll examine that doctrine in this chapter.

Justification can be defined as "the act of divine grace which restores the sinner to the relationship with God that he would have had if he had not sinned."[1] A common phrase used to describe justification is "just as if I'd never sinned." And indeed, that describes it well. When we are justified, God looks at us as if we'd never sinned. We are clean before Him. Jesus' redemptive blood covers us, and God sees only that and not the sin in our lives.

Being justified can also be called our position in Christ: we are without sin. That entitles us to be His children, to be empowered by His Spirit, to enjoy the blessings and benefits of being His children, along with the fulfillment of countless promises in the Bible. We cannot lose this position as His children because it is truly a "once for all" kind of situation. And all this shows us that God is totally content with us: He accepts us and loves us just as we are, even in our sinfulness.

Our contentment must be founded in this position of justification. When we understand that the Lord is totally content with us, we can begin learning to be content with ourselves. There is nothing, absolutely nothing, we can do to make ourselves more acceptable to Almighty God. In His eyes, we are perfect. This saying is so true: "There is nothing you can do to make God love you more; there is nothing you can do to make Him love you less." You cannot earn any more grace and favor with Him than you already have.

Because of this, we can breathe a big sigh of contentment. We no longer need to strive to be accepted by Him. We no longer have to plead for His forgiveness. He will eagerly forgive in a moment at our asking. As Christians, we can be content that we are truly accepted by God.

The Difference Between
Contentment and Satisfaction

You may be asking, "Doesn't God expect me to do better and better in my life as I relate to people and situations?" Yes, He does. But our performance comes under a different area than our position in Christ: it is the area of practice. In our practice, we do know sin, hurt, rebellion, and a lack of the fruit of the Spirit. This is the area in which we need the empowering of the Holy Spirit so that we can progress in the way God wants us to live.

I'd like to share an idea that will help us understand how this works: God is content with our position, but He is not satisfied with who we are at this point in time. He will continue to work in our practice for as long as we live. He knows our final fulfillment, for "He who began a good work in you will perfect it until the day of Christ Jesus" (Philippians 1:6). The Christian life is not a striving for perfection in our performance, but a process of growth as we learn to let the Spirit within direct our desires and plans. God's desire is to see us growing closer to Him.

Remember that we defined contentment as being happy enough with what we have or what we are not to desire something more or different. That describes God's relationship with us through justification in Jesus Christ. He is happy enough with us as His children and doesn't desire anything more in our position than the fact that we've been restored to fellowship with Him.

The word *satisfy,* in contrast, refers to fulfilling our needs, expectations, wishes, or desires. In our walk, in our practice, God is not satisfied for us to remain as we are. He wants us to "excel still more" (1 Thessalonians 4:1). God exhorts us to keep adding qualities that will enrich our relationship with Him and our interaction with others. As James Mackintosh said, "It is right to be contented with what we have, never with what we are." We never totally fulfill all the expectations and wishes of our Father that relate to our practice of Christianity. Nevertheless, He does want us to be content with who we are "in Christ" (our spiritual position).

It is important to understand this distinction between contentment and satisfaction if we are to be truly content. If we can recognize the difference between being content and being satisfied, then we can be content with who we are and at the same time not be satisfied with our daily walk. We can grow more content even while recognizing, "I still have a long way to go while the Spirit of God is busy conforming me more and more into the image of Jesus."

Joyce was confused at first when I explained the difference between contentment and satisfaction. But as we talked, she began to understand. "You mean," she queried, "I can be content with the level of maturity I've achieved so far and yet, at the same time, know that the Lord will continue to work in me to make me better?"

"Exactly," I replied. I went on to clarify that our contentment will make us open to God's working. When we aren't content, we put ourselves down for not being better. We focus so much on ourselves that we're not open to God's continued molding of our reactions, desires, attitudes, etc.

"So in other words," she concluded, "I don't have to feel guilty for feeling content. As long as I desire to continue growing, that's the important part, right?"

"Right," I assured her.

You, too, can experience a contentment that still allows for God's shaping of your character and Christian walk. You can do that by giving God the praise for the growth that has already occurred in your life. Take encouragement from that growth. Be happy with your progress and find peace in it. Stop tearing yourself down for not yet achieving perfection. Focus on the Lord's promises and trust that He'll continue to "work in you, both to will and to work for His good pleasure" (Philippians 2:13). Because He will.

NOTES: 1. *The New Compact Topical Bible* (Grand Rapids: Zondervan Publishing Company, 1972), page 275.

4
Contentment in Being Me

Do you like yourself? Are you content with the body, the temperament, and the personality you have? Unless you've become content with who you are, you probably won't be able to be content with your circumstances. Being content with who you are lays the foundation for contentment with what is happening around you.

That has certainly been true in my life. As a little girl growing up in Norwalk, California, I didn't like myself. I just wasn't content with my life. In those days I had what was called an inferiority complex. Today it's called low self-esteem. And that phrase described my outlook exactly. I didn't esteem myself. I didn't value myself, and as a result, I was discontented with everything in my life.

Several factors contributed to this discontent. One day in third grade after recess, my classmates and I were lining up to march back into our room. Roberta, another third-grade girl, came up behind me, jerked the foursquare ball out of my hands, and started running across the asphalt playground. That made me mad. I chased after her. I caught up with her, swung at her back with my hand, missed, and fell face down onto the asphalt.

When I woke up, the nurse took me into the office and called my mother. She arrived, took one look at my bloodied mouth and gasped. My two front permanent teeth were now only sharp points, shattered by the impact on the playground.

After several trips to the dentist, my smile consisted of two silver capped front teeth that accompanied me through the rest of elementary school. Because of my embarrassment and the ridicule of my peers, I learned to hide my teeth by never smiling fully. Years later when my mouth had finished growing, I received white, permanent caps. Then I had to learn to smile all over again because the muscles of my mouth had trained my upper lip to never reveal my front teeth.

Other areas of my body also made it difficult for me to be content. In junior high when all the other girls seemed to be developing, my chest stayed as flat as ever. I was embarrassed in gym class. Where my chest failed to proceed in front of me, though, my nose seemed to compensate. I thought I had one of the biggest noses around. As far as I was concerned, when people looked at my face, all they could see was my nose. I definitely wasn't content with my body.

I also found it hard to be content with my temperament, even though I grew up with supportive parents. I knew they loved me, but then parents are supposed to love you no matter what. I knew *they* loved me, but I couldn't love myself.

In those growing-up years, I experienced a persistent, uneasy feeling of dissatisfaction with what I did and who I was. If I said something a certain way, I sensed that I should have said it differently. If I reacted a certain way toward someone, I realized later that I should have responded differently. I was never pleased with my performance. Something always should have been either better or different. Years later when I studied the temperaments and discovered that I had a melancholy temperament, I understood why I felt the way I did. I was a perfectionist and nothing met my unrealistic expectations for myself.

Besides my perfectionism, I also thought I was too sensitive. Whenever I watched a sad movie or, for that matter, even a touching commercial, tears would cascade down my cheeks no matter how much I tried to stop them.

Not only was I not content with my temperament, I also wished for a different personality. Although I had several good friends, what I really wanted was to be one of the popular girls in school. But my personality didn't seem to draw the popular kids. If a boy talked to me, I got all tongue-tied. If someone told a joke in class, it seemed like I was the only one who didn't understand (even though I laughed). When I walked in front of a group of boys, I became so tense that my legs stiffened. I was sure they snickered behind my back about my funny walk.

One day Chris, one of the popular girls, started talking to me. I couldn't believe it. As soon as she took a breath, I started rambling on about anything I could think of, ecstatic to finally have her attention. It wasn't until several moments later that I noticed her bored expression. At my next breath, she politely excused herself and left. I mentally hit myself again for blowing my big chance to be accepted by someone popular. I continued to daydream about being witty and "in with the in crowd." I was confident that if I could just become popular, I would finally be content.

These factors—my body, temperament, and personality—all created a great deal of discontent in me. Most of the time I wanted to be someone else. Anyone but me.

These reactions are common among kids, and looking back, I'm sure that my peers, whom I admired so much, experienced similar feelings. But I didn't know that then, so my dissatisfaction with my life continued for many years.

While I was a senior in high school, I started dating Larry and was surprised when he seemed genuinely interested in me. Me? We decided to attend each other's churches. At Larry's church, I accepted Christ as my personal Savior and became a Christian. Almost three years later, we were married in that little church.

But I still wasn't content with being me. Now I was comparing myself with other Christians, and found myself lacking. I believed that if I could just be more like them, I'd be content. I still came away from conversations thinking, "Kathy, why did you say that?" and "I bet they think I'm not spiritual." The gnawing feeling in the pit of my stomach was still there, reminding me often, "I don't like me. When am I ever going to be who I want to be?" It seemed impossible that I would ever be content with myself.

Then in 1978, Larry and I attended a couples' retreat. For the first time, I heard the phrase, "God doesn't make junk!" "Well, of course, He doesn't," I thought, ". . . except for me!" I wanted to believe that catchy little phrase, but how could I when I judged my body, personality, and temperament to be junky?

God's Wisdom

Later, I was confronted with the Scripture that said, "For Thou didst form my inward parts; Thou didst weave me in my mother's womb. I will give thanks to Thee, for I am fearfully and wonderfully made; wonderful are Thy works, and my soul knows it very well. My frame was not hidden from Thee, when I was made in secret, and skillfully wrought in the depths of the earth. Thine eyes have seen my unformed substance; and in Thy book they were all written, the days that were ordained for me, when as yet there was not one of them" (Psalm 139:13-16).

These verses told me that God had supervised my construction: my nose, my frame, my temperament, and my personality. Since He was the architect of my building, if I was going to call myself junky then I was calling God's handiwork junky. In His wisdom, God had made me a certain way to fulfill His special plan for me.

I had never looked at it that way before. And I didn't want to call God's work junky even though I did seem junky to me! I had to decide whether I would continue in my present way of thinking or accept myself—my body and my being—and start choosing contentment with who I was. I determined to accept myself as I was, and I've never regretted it. I now like myself. I like who I am.

But this too was a process. Even after making that initial decision to accept myself, old thought patterns would frequently recur. When I undressed with Larry in the room, my self-esteem would begin to shrivel and I'd think, "How in the world can he say he loves this body? I wish I were better developed." Almost immediately I'd recognize the "old junky thought" and correct myself. "No, Kathy, God made your body and Larry accepts it. Thank You, Lord, that You've made me the way I am. Help me to keep myself in as good of shape as possible."

Even though I corrected my mind, the *feelings* of "junkiness" didn't always go away immediately. I had to tell myself not to operate my life upon my feelings but on the facts I knew to be true. As the years went by, I could more easily reject those "junky" thoughts and think of myself the way God wanted me to. Sometimes the inadequate feelings persisted, but they didn't steal my contentment.

Now, I look at myself honestly and see how God has used my flaws and weaknesses to mold me into someone who is growing into the image of His Son. My physical imperfections have helped to make me more sensitive to the needs of others. I'm more accepting of others, knowing I'm not perfect. Although I still don't enjoy shopping for bathing suits, I've accepted the fact that my body is what it is. And I'm also content with my nose. I do put a lighter foundation on it because it gets more sun than the rest of my face, but I now know people aren't staring at it. Even if they do, it doesn't matter because I like who I am. I'm me, and there isn't anyone else I'd rather be.

For those of us who struggle with being content with who we are, the Bible talks about several godly people who had to learn to be content with who they were. One of them was that well-known fellow, Moses. Moses had many "handicaps" in his life that caused discontent: his quick temper, his stuttering, and his inferiority complex.

After God told Moses that He wanted him to lead the Israelites out of captivity, Moses said, "Who am I, that I should go to Pharaoh, and that I should bring the sons of Israel out of Egypt?" (Exodus 3:11). Moses said to God, "Please, Lord, I have never been eloquent, neither recently nor in time past, nor since Thou hast spoken to Thy servant; for I am slow of speech and slow of tongue" (Exodus 4:10).

Moses wasn't content with himself. And because of his inadequacies, he didn't want to serve God. He wanted to be an eloquent spokesman who was able to enthrall the Israelites and Pharaoh with beautiful words before he was willing to serve God. He wanted to get trained in Toastmasters before he considered himself acceptable and available for God.

But God wanted to take him through His own brand of Toastmaster training. Besides, God was already content to use him the way he was. God wanted to overcome those handicaps by using Moses regardless of his inadequacies rather than allowing him to rely on the human ability he thought he should have. Fortunately, Moses agreed to obey and serve God even in his discontent, and he became more confident and content as he grew in God's power.

Maybe you're like Moses and I used to be: never content with your body, personality, or temperament. Maybe you often compare yourself with others and desire to be like someone else. That's discontent. That's calling what God has made junky!

You can change your discontent into contentment in the area of your physical and inner being. It will be a process of learning "not to think more highly of [yourself] than [you] ought to think; but to think so as to have sound judgment, as God has allotted to each a measure of faith" (Romans 12:3). Sound judgment requires looking at yourself honestly, seeing your abilities and liabilities, accepting those things that can't be changed, and trusting God to change those things that can be altered.

I'd like to suggest some steps you can take to become content with who you are.

1. Ask God's forgiveness for your discontent. Recognize your dissatisfaction with His creation as sin. God assures us in His Word that "If we confess our sins, He is faithful and righteous to forgive us our sins and to cleanse us from all unrighteousness" (1 John 1:9).

2. Make a list of the things you don't like about yourself. Be honest and write down anything you haven't completely accepted about yourself. (Of course, "acceptance" doesn't rule out making some changes you have control over, such as changing eating habits to lose excess weight or wearing

makeup to cover an obvious skin flaw.)

3. Choose to thank the Lord for each of the inadequacies that you've written down. This may not be easy. It may require a choice on your part if it doesn't "feel" good. But you can choose to do this, and your feelings will follow in time.

4. Look for the possible reasons God made you the way you are. Usually, positive character traits have been developed through the "imperfections" you see. If you've become bitter and resentful instead, you can turn your negative attitudes around to become a testimony of God's working. To begin to do that, write down one or more blessings that have resulted from your physical, temperament, or personality flaws.

5. Every time you are reminded of your weak point, choose to praise God for it and for your life. Just because you've praised God once, though, doesn't mean you're never going to think negatively again. You'll focus on your flaw a lot at first, but as you choose to take "every thought captive to the obedience of Christ" (2 Corinthians 10:5), little by little the attention on it will diminish. And especially if you use it as an opportunity to praise the Lord, even Satan won't bring it to your remembrance.

The important thing is to not allow that negative feeling to wipe out your acceptance of your flaw. Each time you sense the "junky feeling" reminding you of an imperfection, choose with your will to override it by thinking, "It's true I'm not completely happy with my nose. Nevertheless, I believe God in His wisdom knew what He was doing when He designed it. Therefore, I won't let my negative feeling about my nose destroy my ability to be content about myself."

As you correct your thinking over time, your area of liability will eventually become less important. Once it does, you'll be freer to reach out to others because your concentration isn't on yourself but on them. And the contentment you experience will show. Then someone will come up to you like a friend did to me and say, "I just love to look at you. You have such a peaceful face." (She didn't even notice my nose!)

5
Contentment During Stress

Ants recently tried to take over my kitchen. At first, two or three ants showed up on my kitchen counter. I didn't take much notice of them, thinking, "Aren't they cute?" Then I remembered how I thought one or two crickets were cute—after all, Jimminy Cricket was cute—until our house started sounding like the great outdoors. Remembering those crickets made me squash those ants. I wasn't going to let them go back to the herd and report what wonderful things they found in Kathy Miller's kitchen.

But even though the herd didn't get the message of their missing-in-action colleagues, they kept coming. I began keeping the kitchen counter and floor as clean as possible.

One night I dreamt that the ants picked up the kitchen and carried it to their ant farm. I went into the kitchen the next morning relieved to find it still there with only one or two ants scouting out the place. They sacrificed their lives.

The next morning the news wasn't as positive. Darcy screamed from the family room, "Mommy, come quick. Ants!"

"Oh, no!" I ran to her side.

"See?" She pointed to a fifteen-foot-long train of ants filing across the tile floor from the wall to a small piece of food and then onto the cat's food. It looked like a view from the Goodyear blimp of the children of Israel crossing the wilderness.

Ten minutes later I had everything cleaned up, thoroughly disgusted that those little critters wouldn't let me keep out one bit of food. So I turned into Mrs. Clean!

Several months have passed now and I'm still very careful to keep the kitchen and family room free from squashed raisins and spilled pineapple juice. At times an ant wanders through, but I think the herd has finally gotten the message: "Kathy Miller has cleaned up her act. You don't need to scout her kitchen anymore."

As I reviewed my battle with the ants, I began to see how stress acts like those ants in our lives. It makes us either clean up our act or become overwhelmed. In the area of contentment, stressful situations either help us become more content or create so much discontent that we're overwhelmed and have a hard time focusing on God.

The dictionary defines stress as "force exerted upon a body that tends to strain or deform its shape." God intends for us to have a spiritual "body" that is shaped in the image of His Son, Jesus: content and trusting God. Stress tries to make that body contort into discontent, distrust, and anxiety. It can manifest itself in our lives in countless ways. Some examples we'll be considering in this chapter are job situations, infertility, unwanted pregnancy, singleness, moving, and materialism. Obviously, we can't consider everything that could possibly be stressful in our lives, but the principles we'll discover can be applied to all kinds of stress.

On the Job

In an article in *Salt and Light*, Connie Arkus wrote, "Finding my mission in life, actively pursuing the 'perfect career' continues to be an elusive dream. During the last two years I've tried a new strategy: asking God for His direction on which career path to follow. I thought this approach was the 'spiritually mature' thing to do! God would then pat me on the head and grant my wish.

"But I continue to wait and wait, and still no answer. I let myself become angry and disappointed with God, doubting His love for me.

"Fortunately, the Holy Spirit recently came to my rescue with Psalm 77. "'Will the Lord reject forever? Will he never show his favor again?'" . . . Then I thought, "To this I will appeal: the years of the right hand of the Most High." I will remember the deeds of the LORD; yes, I will remember your miracles of long ago' (verses 7,10-11, NIV)."

Connie experienced the struggle between contentment and discontent as she looked for satisfaction on the job. She quit her job and returned to a position she held at age nineteen. Although she wasn't completely happy there, she could see benefits: steady income, flexible work schedule, and hours that allowed her to attend her church's Wednesday night service. But she still felt discontented.

She prayed, "I'm not happy with my current job situation. I feel as if I'm taking a big step back. I also feel that I should be lining up more interviews, but with whom and where? Then I remember feeling the unmistakable, overpowering, protective presence of God. Suddenly, I heard Him say that I was exactly where He wanted me to be at the moment and to be content with where I am."[1]

I can relate to Connie's discontent. I worked for seven years at a job I hated. I vacillated between contentment and discontent continually, being fully convinced that God wanted me there yet being fully dissatisfied to be there. Every day I prayed, "God, please help me accept the job You've given me and be content." But by the end of the day I again felt discontented.

Yet I could see God using me there. Several of my coworkers deepened their trust in God because I shared my faith. I wondered, "God, how can You be using me when I'm so discontented with Your will?" My attitude was, "God can't use me unless I'm perfect."

My struggle continued, but the years spent at that job were beneficial in other ways. I thought, "I'll try memorizing Scripture. Maybe that will help me become more obedient to God." Each day I used one of my fifteen-minute coffee breaks to memorize Scripture. I started with Romans 12 and as I reviewed "present your bodies a living and holy sacrifice, acceptable to God, which is your spiritual service of worship," I found my heart a little more "dead to myself"— willing to accept God's plan for me. But I still continued to experience times of discontent.

During that time, I realized I really wanted to have a family—not a job outside the home. Larry and I had been married two years and I was having difficulty becoming pregnant. I thought, "If I were just more content with my job, God would reward me with a baby." Time passed and I didn't grow more content and I didn't conceive, either. A rash developed on my hand that itched constantly. I knew it was caused by anxiety and wondered if I was going crazy.

I wish I could say I gained total contentment when I

finally became pregnant with Darcy two years later, but I can't. I did gain a measure of it, but not the complete contentment I thought I should have.

Maybe it's your job that creates discontent in you. You may often pray for release from your unhappiness, which makes you feel unfulfilled and empty. Maybe like Connie, you feel like God doesn't love you anymore because He hasn't provided that "perfect" career.

Take heart as you meditate on Psalm 77: "Will the Lord reject forever? Will he never show his favor again?" (NIV). The obvious answer to those questions is, "No, He will not reject me forever, and actually He has never rejected me. It's just that He seems at a distance right now. He does love me and someday I'll sense His love again."

As you struggle during this time, can you see anything good coming from it? Can you trust God that Romans 8:28 is true: "all things . . . work together for good to those who love God, to those who are called according to His purpose"? And can you give up your perfectionist expectations that say, "I must be totally content or else I'm not pleasing God"?

God *is* working contentment in you, and He is already pleased if you're making progress.

At the same time, it could be that your discontent is God's way of making you look for a different job. Continue to pray for His direction and He will lead you.

To Be Single or Married?

Jeri is in her mid-thirties and single. She prays almost every day for God to send Mr. Right. She asks all her friends to set her up for a date with any bachelor they know. It's very difficult for her to consider that God may want her to remain single. She has always wanted to be a wife.

Now you might envision Jeri as a "nerd." But the truth is, she's a vivacious Christian woman who is great fun to be with and makes people feel loved and important. It's a mystery to me why some handsome guy hasn't grabbed her tight and not let go.

Why does God choose certain people to be single and others to be married? I don't know. But I do know this is an area that can produce much discontent in a life. Yet it can also be an area of great contentment.

Luci Swindoll finds single life happy, rich, fun, fulfilling . . . even preferred. The sister of Chuck Swindoll says, "As a little girl, I always liked the idea of a single lifestyle. I had high goals. I wanted to sing professionally. I wanted to travel. I realized that if I married, I wouldn't have time to accomplish those goals. I accepted Christ as my Savior at age thirteen, and shortly after that I told a girlfriend that I didn't ever want to marry. Yet I never thought those who wanted to marry were weird. This was my calling and that was theirs."

Yet Luci was still very aware of pressure to marry from those around her. She was even engaged as a freshman in college but realized she was being manipulated by her mother and broke off the engagement.

Since then, she has lived a fulfilling and content life. At times she comes across singles who also want to remain that way. To them she advises, "Stick to your guns. Ask the Lord for His leadership and fill your life with meaningful activity. Often the pressure to marry comes from unhappily married people who think the single person ought to be in the same unhappy boat they are in. But I also tell them they should think through their decision to remain unmarried very carefully."

But more often Luci counsels those who are discontent to be single. Then she says, "Make the very most of your single life, trusting God for a mate. If He doesn't send one, stop bemoaning your fate. You can live life to the full instead of waiting for the better to come along, because the better is life itself. If you get more involved in life, you have something more to offer a spouse."[2]

If you are single but want to be married, Luci's advice is for you. If you're unhappily married, we'll be dealing with that problem in our chapter on relationships . . . so hold on.

The Absence . . . or Abundance of the Joys of Motherhood

Because of a hysterectomy, my friend Julie's long-held desire to be a birth mother will never be reality. In the past, she and her husband were foster parents and tried to adopt two little girls, but they were denied permission.

Julie shares, "God is faithful regardless of my circumstances. I can choose to be content by working through the feelings of discontent. I do that by talking and journaling.

"I'm fairly content until I hear a mother complain about her children. Interestingly enough, since my hysterectomy, it's been easier for me to be content. When there was the possibility of conceiving, I hoped God would answer my prayers. But now, I've been able to accept God's plan more readily. I still struggle but it's less painful."

Julie has seen God's provision of "substitute" children. He has given her a job working with school children. She says this daily contact with children gives her joy she would have received from her own children.

As I listened to Julie's story of childlessness, I thought of Psalm 37:4: "Delight yourself in the LORD; and He will give you the desires of your heart." It seems Julie does delight herself in God, so why hasn't He granted her heart's desire? Well, if I knew that answer, I'd most likely be asked to teach seminary.

But I do know God is faithful regardless of unhappy circumstances and unfulfilled desires. In time, maybe God will give Julie children in a way she can't even imagine now.

My friend Sue gave birth for the first time after twenty years of marriage, during which she never used any birth control.

Truly, Isaiah 55:8-9 is still true: "'For My thoughts are not your thoughts, neither are your ways My ways,' declares the LORD. 'For as the heavens are higher than the earth, so are My ways higher than your ways, and My thoughts than your thoughts.'" Reading that can either make us angry and bitter or trusting and content—it's up to us.

We've talked about not being able to have children. Now let's look into the life of a woman who was devastated when she conceived her third. Maradi's children were fifteen and thirteen when she discovered she was pregnant at thirty-eight years of age. She felt shocked and betrayed. "'Lord, why are You doing this? I'm too old. My life is over . . . ruined. I don't want this baby.' I felt guilty for thinking like that and was completely discontent.

"My husband, Ted, asked me, 'Have you thanked the Lord for the baby?' So I prayed, 'Lord, You know I'm not thankful. But Your Word says I'm to be. Please help me.' God seemed to answer, 'I don't make mistakes. This child has always been in My plans. I just didn't let you in on it.' As I concentrated on Psalm 139 and chose to thank God, a love for the baby began to grow."

Michael was born in 1984, and he became the joy of the family. Maradi says, "My concept of God's sovereignty has grown. I try to view life through God's eyes. He sees the overall picture. He knew our family needed Michael to get us through the teenaged years of our older children. Michael's a ray of sunshine. I couldn't be more content to have him as a part of our family."

If you're unexpectedly pregnant, wondering how you'll ever live through another child, take a clue from Maradi. There can be contentment even adding another family member.

Moving

Dana missed her hometown tremendously. She and her husband and their three children were forced to move to New Mexico when her husband's employer transferred him.

"I didn't feel like I belonged there. It wasn't home. I felt like I'd been displaced. I got to the point of thinking that if I couldn't be in Montana, I wouldn't be happy anywhere! And life was indeed miserable. My oldest son, Brent, constantly asked when we could move back to Montana. He'd even cry himself to sleep at night. It broke my heart and I know my husband was sad about it, too, but his job required us to be in New Mexico.

"Trying to cheer up Brent actually helped me to adjust and become more content. I'm still not completely happy about being here, but I'm learning. When I'd try to point out some positives to Brent, I guess I convinced myself it wasn't so bad after all. But because my tendency to get depressed is still there, I have to make the decision to dwell on how God has blessed us here. I've grown closer to the Lord because of my loneliness. We're part of a wonderful church and have met some precious Christians. Believe me, it's taken a lot of prayer to even begin to be content. But God has answered. Even Brent has become happier. His best friend moved away recently and I wondered whether that would throw him back into the pits, but it didn't. He soon found a new best friend and that showed me he'd finally adjusted.

"The level of contentment I've achieved is a result of realizing I must live life one day at a time, and today is not forever. Who knows? Maybe someday we'll move back to Montana and I'll be homesick for New Mexico. In the meantime, I've also learned to be patient with myself. At first I thought I should become perfectly content immediately after moving here. Now I know I must grow and change over a period of time. It's more painful that way, but I've cooperated with God's healing process rather than pretending I love it here and covering up my feelings."

Few things are more stressful than pulling up roots and adjusting to a whole new life in a new location. Many of the things we look to for stability and happiness are suddenly left behind. But when our need for fresh contentment is greatest, God will come through. He'll teach us new ways to open ourselves to Him and to our surroundings so that longed-for contentment can flourish.

Materialism

I opened the letter out of curiosity. It began: "Dear Kathy Miller: Congratulations! You've been approved for our prestigious credit card with a $5,000 line of credit. Obviously, you're among a small select group of successful people who've earned the good life—who deserve all of the credit and special privileges our credit card gives."

Lucky me! I could hardly contain myself thinking I had so much money available to me. And to think they thought of me as successful! Well, now, how could I possibly be discontented knowing that?

The truth of the matter is, materialism creates and feeds discontent in many people, Christians included. After all, who doesn't want to earn the good life? Seeking that good life is expected by society. If you don't, you aren't valuable and "contributing."

An article in the *Wall Street Journal* about young executives gives us insight into what the good life requires. "Tony James is so intense that he charters Learjets at 5 a.m. for business meetings. David Lakhdhir puts so much time into his job that he has hung up a photo of his college crew team to remind himself what free time was like. And Tom Steyer worries that his job is so demanding that he won't have time for a honeymoon when he gets married this summer.

"These are some of the 'whiz kids' who breezed through schools like Harvard, Yale and Stanford a few years ago. Today, they work 80-hour weeks in Wall Street's takeover business—and worry that that still isn't enough."[3]

Unfortunately, this "good life" isn't "enjoyed" only by the adults. In another *Wall Street Journal* article, Jeffrey Zaslow writes, "With an almost Orwellian eeriness, giant photos of teen-age boys and girls peer out over Crestwood Plaza here, where shoppers hurry in and out of fashion boutiques and stores piled high with trendy merchandise.

"To Jennifer Hunt, the atmosphere in malls like this is intoxicating. 'I see something. I fall in love with it. I have to have it,' the 15-year-old says. 'My mother says I'm—what's the word? Insatiable.'"[4]

No wonder Christians have a hard time being content when so much discontent surrounds them. Joan identifies materialism as her area of greatest discontent. "I have a hard time deciding what my needs and wants truly are. God's power can supply my needs but maybe what I think my needs are, in reality, are wants. A person can be content if their needs are being met, but if they can't define their needs, they can't be content.

"I was raised by parents who went through the depression. My mother was often anxious about material things. I've noticed that my children are careless about their possessions. They have an 'easy come, easy go' attitude, which is the opposite of my parents' attitude. I'm in the middle, trying to have a balanced perspective."

Defining the difference between needs and wants can be significant in helping us as Christian women to be content in a world that says, "Have it your way," and "You deserve the best."

Christian psychologist Larry Crabb says, "Because people are both physical beings and personal beings, they have both physical needs and personal needs. Physical needs consist of whatever is needed to physically survive, to keep the body alive—food, clothing, shelter, etc. Personal needs consist of whatever is required to personally survive, to keep the person alive—significance and security as a basis for self-worth."[5]

Crabb says that we must "differentiate between *needs* and *wants*. We *need* significance and security in order to persevere in faithful living. We may *want* approval, money, fame, recognition . . . etc., etc. And I may passionately want them to the point where their absence provokes a nonsinful legitimate pain of excruciating proportions. But I do not *need* any of them in order to be a whole person who can live biblically."[6]

Philippians 4:19 promises, "My God shall supply all your needs according to His riches in glory in Christ Jesus." We nod our agreement but we may have a different definition of needs than God does. And at the time, we're completely convinced that we're right.

There have been many times when I've thought, "Once the new drapes get installed, my living room will be complete and I'll be content. Once the kids are gone to school all day, then I'll be content." The list goes on and on.

How about you? Think of something you once wanted very much and received. Does it still make you happy? Or has it lost its "punch"? Now think of something you once longed for and didn't receive. Have you somehow been able to continue living your life with some level of joy?

The call of material things is like that. They beckon us, make us discontented, and even if they arrive in our lives, they quickly lose their significance.

Pastor Kevin Budd of Redeemer Covenant Church, Downey, California, gives this analysis: "I want to speak of a spiritually significant tendency that all humans seem to possess: fixation. I mean by 'fixation' that unbelievable human tendency to focus in on one [thing] . . . and lose all sense of its relative unimportance in light of the overall functioning of the universe. . . . When we lose perspective about circumstances, we sacrifice our contentment, and receive nothing of value in return.

"The New Testament tells us that every good gift comes to us from God, and that He does not tease us with His gifts, giving us boulders in place of bread, or serpents in place of seafood. But if that is true, why are we so often dissatisfied with what we have received? Why do we find ourselves seeking more, more, more?

"Let me encourage you, when you hear yourself saying 'if only,' to determine then and there to fix your eyes on Jesus and the many gifts He has given, confessing to God your ungrateful and selfish attitude, and wait for Him to make you content even without that desired object or situation. If we are going to fixate, let it be upon Jesus."

Yes, that's the solution. Fixing our eyes on Jesus, trusting that God knows what our true needs are. If I don't receive that "something" that seems so necessary, maybe it's not truly a need in my life.

Paul spelled out for us what our true needs are: "We have brought nothing into the world, so we cannot take anything out of it either. And if we have food and covering, with these we shall be content" (1 Timothy 6:7-8).

In Philippians 3:8, Paul gives us another perspective that will help us gain contentment: "I count all things to be loss in view of the surpassing value of knowing Christ Jesus my Lord, for whom I have suffered the loss of all things, and count them but rubbish in order that I may gain Christ."

How can we be content with the lack or abundance of material things? By realizing that possessions are as valuable as the trash in our wastebasket in comparison to the worth of knowing Christ Jesus as our Lord and Savior.

We can pray along with Gotthold Ephraim Lessing, "My God, give me neither poverty nor riches, but what-soever it may be Thy will to give, give me with a heart that knows humbly to acquiesce in what is Thy will."

In Proverbs 30:7-9, a wise man named Agur said similarly, "Two things I ask of you, O LORD; do not refuse me before I die: keep falsehood and lies far from me; give me neither poverty nor riches, but give me only my daily bread. Otherwise, I may have too much and disown you and say, 'Who is the LORD?' Or I may become poor and steal, and so dishonor the name of my God" (NIV).

The Israelites and God's Faithfulness

As we think about our true needs and wants, whether that applies to being married or unmarried, having children or being barren, enjoying a job or suffering through it, being rich or poor, contentment is something we choose to have as we concentrate on God's faithfulness to supply our true needs. Unfortunately, the Israelites didn't do that, and so they are an example of what to avoid. Starting in Exodus and continuing through Numbers, in different situations, the Israelites didn't believe God wanted their best.

In Exodus 15-17, we see that they complained about thirst and hunger. God provided water and food. Yet they never seemed to learn their lesson: God would provide what they truly needed. He had worked miracles to deliver them from bondage in Egypt, yet they still couldn't believe that He loved them. He had saved them from the angel of death at the Passover, yet they couldn't believe that He wanted to bless them. He had parted the Red Sea, yet they couldn't believe He had the power to provide for them. Even though they disobeyed and distrusted Him, He continued to be faithful in providing for their true needs.

Can you and I learn from the Israelites that we can trust God to be faithful and thus gain contentment? Habakkuk 3:17-18 gives us a principle to follow:

> Though the fig tree should not blossom,
> And there be no fruit on the vines,
> Though the yield of the olive should fail,
> And the fields produce no food,
> Though the flock should be cut off from the fold,
> And there be no cattle in the stalls,
> Yet I will exult in the LORD,
> I will rejoice in the God of my salvation.

Do you notice a pattern in these verses? It goes like this: "Though _____ and _____, though _____ and _____, though _____ and _____, yet I will _____, I will _____."

We can apply the same pattern in our lives to turn from discontent to contentment as we live in a stressful world. We need to substitute into those verses whatever areas of discontent we struggle with and say:

> "Though I want children and can't get pregnant;
> Though I'm not married and want to be a wife;
> Though I don't like my job and can't find a
>   satisfying one;
> Yet I will exult in God's faithfulness,
> I will rejoice in God, who wants the best for me
>   and promises to meet my needs."

By applying this "Though _____ I will" principle, we can turn our minds from those things that cause our discontent and begin to "fixate" on God's faithfulness. Concentrating on His desire to help me in stressful situations will encourage my trust in Him to grow. This, also, is a process of changing my thinking from distrust ("God can't help me in this stressful circumstance") to trust ("I don't know how He'll do it, and it's even hard for me to believe He will, but I'm going to ask for and expect God's help and strength during this time").

One evening, my sister, Karen, and her three-year-old daughter, Kelly, were at my home. After they left, I discovered Kelly's shoes and clothes in our bathroom were she had taken a bath. I called Karen so she wouldn't search for them frantically the next morning. After she hung up, Karen told Kelly her clothes and shoes were at Aunt Kathy's house. Kelly replied, "Don't worry, Mommy, Kathy will take good care of them."

Sister in Christ, be content, God will take good care of you even in stressful circumstances. You can be content knowing that.

(By the way, the ants are now in my *bathroom*! Ants—and stress—never give up!)

NOTES: 1. Connie Arkus, "Discovering Miracles," *Salt and Light* (June/July 1987), pages 1, 5, used by permission.
2. Luci Swindoll, from an interview, *Today's Christian Woman* (January/February 1984), pages 66-67.
3. George Anders, Paul Blustein, and Patricia Gray (Staff Reporters), "Merger Whiz Kids," *Wall Street Journal* (June 2, 1986), page 1.
4. Jeffrey Zaslow, "Children's Search for Values Leading to Shopping Malls," *Wall Street Journal* (March 13, 1987), page 1.
5. Larry J. Crabb, Jr., *Effective Biblical Counseling* (Grand Rapids: The Zondervan Corporation, 1977), page 114, used by permission.
6. Crabb, *Effective Biblical Counseling,* page 116, used by permission.

6
Contentment During Trials

I walked into my sleeping son's room and gently laid my hand on his shoulder. "Honey, time to wake up." Ten-year-old Mark groggily rolled over and tried unsuccessfully to open his eyes. "Mark, it's time to get ready for school. Which pants do you want to wear today? I'll get them out."

As I moved over to the dresser, my eyes focused on the tarantula's cage. Something looked different. My mind finally comprehended what was wrong and I gasped, "Oh, no, the tarantula's dead. He's upside down."

Mark bolted up in bed. I fled the room, fighting back tears. "Why am I crying over a stupid dead spider?" I questioned. "Because I killed it. I've been meaning to check his water. Maybe he got dehydrated. Oh no, I killed him!"

I ran into the bedroom where Larry slept. "Larry, the tarantula's dead. He's upside down. I forgot to refill his water dish. I feel so bad."

Larry jumped out of bed. "Maybe he's molting."

After a few minutes of examination, Larry declared, "He's alive. He's just begun his molt."

That day, we watched the tarantula closely. This was our first experience with molting. Mark's tarantula book told us that molting renews the tarantula's outer covering and can even replace "missing parts." Unless a tarantula molts, it won't be able to grow. It sounded like a painful process to me.

That evening, Mark called from his bedroom, "The tarantula is out of his skin." We ran to see, and there were now two spiders in the cage. His old skin lay discarded in one corner and a "new" spider lay beside it, looking exhausted. He had lived through his transformation and was now slightly bigger and shiny-looking. We had witnessed one of God's intriguing creations: the molting of a tarantula.

Thinking of that experience, I realized how much a tarantula's molting can apply to trials. Trials bring a painful process that results in greater dependence on God. Whether that painful process is happening to someone else or to ourselves, we can grow in our ability to be content and believe that God is still in control. He is the sovereign God of this universe—even when He allows unhappy circumstances like tragedy, death, persecution, and suffering.

Death

How can anyone be content when faced with death, especially the death of a loved one? This is a hard question, requiring the assurance that God is indeed supreme.

In July 1987, four Christian men were killed in a plane crash after leaving a Montana ranch where they'd attended a week-long retreat with other supporters of Dr. James Dobson's ministry, Focus on the Family. Hugo Schoellkopf, Dr. Trevor Mabery, Rev. Creath Davis, and George Clark were strong Christian leaders who would seem to be God's last choice for an untimely death. How could God allow such a tragedy? How could the bereaved families reconcile such a shock?

These are the questions any thoughtful person will ponder when hearing of calamities. Yet God's sovereignty can be trusted and must be believed—that is the basis for contentment in the midst of trials. That doesn't mean there aren't times of disbelief, anger, bargaining, and other stages of grief that are necessary. It's just that underlying the natural reactions of feelings, there is the deep knowledge that God is in control.

And it's that kind of knowledge that enabled seven sons of those four men to fly to the area where their fathers died—just hours after the crash site was found. As they flew by the crash site, they bowed their heads in prayer, dedicating themselves to the Lord.

At the memorial service, Dr. James Dobson said, "Would you have enjoyed being there when those men made the transition to the other side? The Lord greeted them and wrapped His arms around them. Creath was laughing, I know he was, and Hugo was talking in that Texas accent that most of us couldn't understand very well.

"Knowing them, as I did, I can hear them saying, 'But Lord, what about our families?' And I know the Lord gave them the assurance that He is going to be with you all—and He will."

After the service, over 3,000 mourners left the church to discover a small but brilliant rainbow appearing directly above the church steeple. One friend remarked, "It was as though the Lord was saying, 'It's okay; everything will be alright. They are with Me now.'"[1]

Knowing that a loved one is with God is one of the keys to an attitude of contentment in the face of death. Luci Shaw can give us several others. She's the widow of Harold Shaw, the late publisher and president of Harold Shaw Publishers in Wheaton, Illinois. When Harold was first diagnosed with lung cancer, Luci prayed with him for his healing. But he died less than sixteen months later.

Luci relates, "When he found out he had cancer, we prayed with friends consistently for his healing and he truly believed he was going to be healed. I wanted to believe, but there's a very narrow line between having ultimate faith for healing and also facing the reality of death and preparing for it. I tried to walk that narrow line and keep the balance."

Even though they wanted his healing, they lived contentment by making practical plans. "He gave me all sorts of wonderful help in preparing for life without him. I'm inexperienced with money, investments, that sort of thing. But he wrote in this little black book, which I called my 'Bible.' He used different pages for car maintenance, the furnace, sources of income, taxes, what our investments were, who to call on if I needed advice for this or that.

"Right after Harold recovered from his first lung surgery, we went and bought a grave site together. I thought it would be a bummer of a day, but it was wonderful. We took a picnic lunch, and went to this little cemetery. We saw what areas were still available, and we found what we wanted and sat there on a slope in the sun, under the beautiful fall foliage and had a picnic. I thought, 'Isn't this neat that we can do this together and know we will someday lie here together?' It was an experience that we would look back to and laugh about and enjoy. It was poignant but not at all morbid or sad.

"Even on the last day of his life when he was so weak that he couldn't speak, he made notes on a scrap of paper about taxes for our accountant so I'd know what to do about them. We spent that whole last day together. I knew death was very close. We tied up all of the loose ends, and expressed all the things we really wanted to say to each other. I'm so sorry for women whose husbands die suddenly so that they don't have that sort of opportunity. My marriage is closed but not unfinished."[2]

That's contentment in action. It's facing the reality of death even while praying for healing. It's planning for a future even when the future seems as dark as storm clouds. And yet contentment isn't happiness and it may not be a sense of satisfaction either.

My friend Annie and I discovered that as we talked about her situation. Her husband, Kyle, is dying of melanoma, the deadliest kind of skin cancer. In his early forties, Kyle has already lived five years longer than doctors predicted. In 1980, he was first diagnosed and surgery was performed. Then the second appearance of a tumor in 1982 caused him to choose an alternative diet therapy, which the Lord used to give a healing. In fact, we all thought he was completely healed. Then in early 1987, a third appearance of the disease struck his body and has now affected his brain.

Kyle and Annie had only known the Lord for about two years when the melanoma was discovered and they depended upon Him with a strong grasp of their faith. But it wasn't easy. The therapy they chose required Annie to be in the kitchen twelve hours a day to prepare special juices and meals. Annie reacted unfavorably to the diet she and her two teenaged children ate along with Kyle. At one point, in her tension, she screamed at her daughters, "If we don't do this, your father will die."

Because of those years of seeing the Lord heal and provide, Kyle and Annie's faith has grown tremendously. Yet Kyle is now to the point where he can barely talk and his mind is affected by the brain tumors. Annie feels like she's alone. She had always depended on Kyle. Now she must make decisions on her own. When I asked her for her definition of contentment, she said, "It's more of a satisfied, happy feeling. I don't feel that I'm content, but I am at peace."

I responded, "Contentment isn't necessarily happiness. There's a difference between contentment and happiness. Happiness is that external feeling that's based upon good circumstances. Contentment, on the other hand, is an inner trusting in God that may not be happy on the outside. You can still shed tears and be content."

She mulled over my comments and said, "Under your definition, I guess I am content. It amazes me how God works. Sometimes it's right from the Word, other times from the radio or books. Then other times He sends human angels—like stepping stones across murky water.

"A week or two ago, I was angry at God and didn't know where He was. Now I'm not angry—I got permission to be angry so I could work through it. I go through different steps repeatedly. Now I'm at acceptance, but that may change.

"When I think I'm at the end, something happens. I get to the other side and I don't know how. That's the rescue of 1 Corinthians 10:13. I can't get strength from Kyle now; I can only get it from God. I have to release Kyle to God. If God doesn't heal, I'll see Kyle up there."

Annie has seen God's provision of contentment in times of trial, even though her emotions continue to fluctuate.

Heartbreak

Bob and Jane Sturm know the meaning of heartbreak. They were booked to leave for Ethiopia as SIM International missionaries in March 1985, but their fourteen-month-old son, John, began to show signs of a dysfunction affecting his speech and development. They put their departure on hold for six months and prayed for God's healing.

Over the following months, a new baby, Mark, was born to the Sturms and John's condition worsened. Eventually the probable cause of John's condition was diagnosed as neuronal ceroid lipafuscinosis, a rare hereditary disease. Its main symptoms are progressive mental deterioration, unsteadiness of movements, visual failure, and arrest of brain growth. The mean age at death is seven years. There is no treatment.

As 1986 passed with no improvement in John, Mark began showing the same signs John had. Bob says, "Needless to say, seeing this in Mark is very hard emotionally. In many ways it's harder than finding out about John. Our hopes that Mark would enjoy a normal life were very high.

"But we're eternally grateful that we know the Lord, and that He can somehow use these little lives for His glory. And we know that they will spend eternity in His presence . . . whole.

"John continues to be a very content little boy. He has continued to regress and is now very floppy and hard to hold. We have pretty well accepted his condition, and though his care involves a lot of time and work, we are happy to serve his needs. Being forced to deal with the possibility of his death has been a time of grieving.

"We still desire very much to serve in Ethiopia. In fact, talking and thinking about that is second only to the grief we feel over our boys. We're so glad we can place these two things which are so very important to us into the Lord's loving hands."[3]

No one expects Bob and Jane Sturm to jump up and down with joy over their heartbreaking circumstances. Yet they are experiencing a contentment that's based on their trust in God's plans for them. It's hard to imagine that God would prevent some willing servants to minister for Him, but He does have different ideas than we sometimes do. We look at life from a temporary vantage point; God has an eternal perspective.

Persecution

On May 16, 1980, Mary Stauffer, a missionary serving with the Baptist General Conference, and her daughter, Beth, were kidnapped in Minnesota and held captive for fifty-two days before escaping. Yet while they were being physically abused and emotionally persecuted, they experienced God's contentment.

Mary says, "I am so grateful that God gave me the resources to be kind to (the kidnapper). It was not within my human strength to love him, but I had to remember that God loved him as much as He loved me. It was for me to pray for him, to share the gospel with him, to show the love of Christ. God gave Beth and me the ability to be kind to that man.

"I did feel despair at times. I asked, 'Why, Lord? What's the use of being a Christian if I can't depend on You to keep me out of things like this?' When I said that, I didn't hear any voice, but the thought came to me, 'Mary, if you don't trust Me, whom are you going to trust?' The Bible says that God is with us, that He is in control. That promise gave us hope.

"We knew that if we were killed, we would go to be with Christ. Beth knew that we had the hope of Heaven. One day she said to me, 'Mom, I don't like to think about this, but in a way it would be better for you and me to die than for (the kidnapper) to die because we'll go to be with Jesus. But if he died, he would go to hell.'

"We have seen God working for His glory through our experience in several ways. People have said to me, 'I think I can go through some kinds of trouble now because I see that the resources that you had from God are the same ones available to me.' They see that I'm not a super-saint, that I'm just like them. God gave me strength, and He will give strength to them.

"The greatest impact was probably on our own families. During the time of the kidnapping, my father, who was 77 years old, made a commitment to Christ. I had been praying for him for more than 30 years. Then, about two weeks after that, (my father-in-law) made a commitment to Christ.

"The temptation to be bitter was real during parts of our captivity. But God reminded me that vengeance belongs to Him. I realized that bitterness and anger are self-destructive. Those feelings destroy us, not the person to whom they are directed."[4]

Mary Stauffer has seen God's "higher thoughts and ways" work and His sovereignty reign. That doesn't mean she's thrilled about the abuse she and her daughter suffered. Instead, she chose to obey God and surrender her negative feelings to Him. That's what is required for contentment: not surrendering to those ungodly feelings that turn into bitterness, anger, and hate; but believing, as Mary did, that "God is in control."

Can't I Grieve?

As we've been discussing some very heavy trials—death, heartbreak, and persecution—it may seem like there isn't room for expressing feelings. But that's not true. Contentment doesn't mean not grieving or expressing emotions. A person can, indeed, express his emotions through tears or sorrow and still be content inside.

In fact, grieving may be necessary as God heals those emotional wounds and continues the process of strengthening contentment in your life. I recently read an article by a woman who recognized this truth after being unable to grieve over her father's death. Kathy Olsen writes, "But during that long first year of sorrow and discouragement, my habit of suppressing emotions was still a strong coping mechanism for me. Some mistook my composure for deep faith and told me how strong I was. That was very flattering, but it merely reinforced a bad habit rather than encouraging faith.

"At the same time a persistent message from my early spiritual training reinforced my habit. Whether intended or not, the message I kept hearing in my mind was that sorrow and strong faith are incompatible."

Kathy learned that this isn't true and discovered a difference between real sorrow and despair or self-pity. "Despair is defined as 'loss of all hope or confidence.' As Christians we need never despair, because our hope and confidence are in the Lord Jesus Christ.

"Self-pity . . . describes excessive sorrow or a continuation of grief long after the grace for recovery has been supplied."[5]

If you are experiencing true sorrow, you can still have a content spirit by believing—even through your tears—that God is in control of your life and that His love will never leave you despairing.

We can agree with William Temple, who said, "Contentment with the divine will is the best remedy we can apply to misfortune."

Joseph

The biblical example of Joseph can be encouraging as we consider how to be content in spite of persecution, misunderstanding, and trials. He was falsely accused of sin and forgotten by someone who owed him a favor. Yet through all of this his trust in God grew and he saw God's hand of favor upon his life.

In similar circumstances, I'm sure that I would have questioned God, saying, "Well, Lord, if You can give me favor with these people, why can't You just go ahead and deliver me? It seems like You're only using Your power halfway. I know You're a powerful God but You're sure not acting like it."

God finally revealed His plan by making Joseph second in command to the Pharaoh, using him to spare many lives during a time of famine.

Then when Joseph's brothers appeared before him, Joseph demonstrated his contentment and trust by saying, "Now, therefore, it was not you who sent me here, but God" (Genesis 45:8).

Joseph's contentment came from believing that God was in control even though men's hands were against him. He acknowledged that God was working His own sovereign plan through people's ungodly decisions.

Later in Genesis when Jacob died, the brothers of Joseph began to wonder whether Joseph had been kind to them only because of their father. They came to him asking for forgiveness again, offering to become his servants.

Joseph responded, "Do not be afraid, for am I in God's place? And as for you, you meant evil against me, but God meant it for good in order to bring about this present result, to preserve many people alive" (Genesis 50:19-20).

Who knows? Whatever trials you are facing may be meant to bring blessing to many. We can certainly find contentment in that.

Prescription for Contentment

Paul gives us a guide for gaining contentment in the midst of trials in Romans 8:18-39.

Verse 18 tells us what our *perspective* should be about trials: "For I consider that the sufferings of this present time are not worthy to be compared with the glory that is to be revealed to us." *I can be content because earthly trials are puny compared to Heaven's eternal glory.*

Verses 24 and 25 tell us about the *puzzle* regarding trials: "For in hope we have been saved, but hope that is seen is not hope; for why does one also hope for what he sees? But if we hope for what we do not see, with perseverance we wait eagerly for it." *I can be content because I don't have to know all the answers and reasons for trials.*

Verses 26 and 27 tell us the *partner* we have during trials: "And in the same way the Spirit also helps our weakness; for we do not know how to pray as we should, but the Spirit himself intercedes for us with groanings too deep for words . . . according to the will of God." *I can be content because the Spirit is praying for me during trials.*

Verse 28 tells us the *purpose* for trials: "And we know that God causes all things to work together for good to those who love God, to those who are called according to His purpose." *I can be content because God will bring something good from trials.*

Verse 32 tells us the *provision* for trials: "He who did not spare His own Son, but delivered Him up for us all, how will He not also with Him freely give us all things?" *I can be content because God will provide everything I truly need for strength and victory during trials.*

Verses 38 and 39 tell us the *protection* we have during trials: "For I am convinced that neither death, nor life, nor angels, nor principalities, nor things present, nor things to come, nor powers, nor height, nor depth, nor any other created thing, shall be able to separate us from the love of God, which is in Christ Jesus our Lord." *I can be content because trials can't separate me from God, even though it doesn't feel like He's there.*

God's Sovereignty

It all boils down to knowing that God is in control, that He is sovereign. Charles Swindoll defines sovereignty as "our all-wise, all-knowing God reigning in realms beyond our comprehension to bring about a plan beyond our ability to alter, hinder, or stop." Within that sovereignty, God determined that man would have free will. Sovereignty doesn't determine which evil act man does but only that he has the ability to do evil.

As you and I go through trials, let's remember that we can be content because God is in control. He's the blessed controller of all things, and He's using everything in our lives to strengthen the new, spiritual man within us. If God weren't in control—if I didn't have the assurance that there is a perspective, partner, purpose, and provision for everything I'm going through—then I'd have every right to be discontent. I'd also be frantic and worried because it would appear that God wasn't going to work everything for my good. In effect, I'd be on my own, with no help or assistance from an impotent God.

But that isn't the case. God is not only in Heaven, but through His Spirit, He can powerfully provide whatever help and strength you and I need—even when trials seem overwhelming. Reminding myself that God is in control and that He cares about what I'm going through helps contentment to grow strong within me. Then I have the attitude the prophet expressed in Jeremiah 29:11: "'For I know the plans that I have for you,' declares the LORD, 'plans for welfare and not for calamity to give you a future and a hope.'"

It's just like Mark's tarantula. God created that spider and its very unique way to grow. He requires it to go through a trial of molting, of shedding its old skin.

As Christians, we also go through a similar transformation during trials when we shed attitudes and perspectives that hinder our relationship with God. We come out on the other side being more willing to depend on God and trust His plan in our lives—which results in greater contentment.

NOTES: 1. James Dobson, "Tragedy in the Absaroka Mountain," *Focus on the Family Magazine* (September 1987), page 3, used by permission.
2. Interview with Luci Shaw by Dale Hanson Bourke, "Luci Shaw: A Life Observed," *Today's Christian Woman*, a *Christianity Today* publication (September/October 1987), pages 83,86, used by permission.
3. Bob and Jane Sturm, "We Haven't Given Up," *SIM Now* (October 1987), pages 4-5.
4. Mary Stauffer, "Kidnapped—Looking Back," *Decision Magazine* (September 1987), pages 14-15, used by permission.
5. Kathy Olsen, "A Time to Mourn," *Discipleship Journal*, Issue 41 (September/October 1987), pages 6-9.

7
Contentment During Troubled Relationships

As I prepared breakfast for two-year-old Darcy, my husband, Larry, announced that he was flying a friend to a distant city for the day.

"Can I go, too?" I begged.

"The plane I've rented is a two-seater, Kathy. Besides, it's too much trouble to take the kids. You stay home and have a nice, relaxing day."

He pecked my cheek with a kiss and turned to go. I followed him down the hall carrying the apple I'd been eating. "You don't understand, Larry. I can't have a 'nice, relaxing day' with a two-year-old and a newborn. I need you here to help me. Sometimes I get really angry. . . ."

"Oh, Kathy, that's just some motherhood blues. You'll be fine. See you tonight."

Larry walked through the laundry room into the garage, closing the door behind him. I stood paralyzed with anger. The closed door seemed to represent the emotional wall between us, although Larry acted as if it weren't there. That made me even more furious.

"How can you be so insensitive to my needs, Larry? Why have you stopped being the wonderful Christian husband I married? Sometimes I hate you!"

My arm snapped back and then forward, hurling the half-eaten apple against the door, where it splattered onto the walls of the laundry room. I picked up the apple core from the floor but didn't clean the apple bits from the walls. Over the next couple of weeks, the dirty walls reminded me of my husband's insensitivity and God's deaf ear to my pleas to change Larry. Unfortunately, my anger spilled onto Darcy, whom I often physically and emotionally abused.

At that point, Larry and I had been married for seven years. It seemed we were headed for the divorce court—or the court where I would be convicted of killing Darcy—I didn't know which would hit first.

Discontent ruled my life at that time, and it was Larry's fault, I reasoned. After all, if he would be the Christian husband and father he should be, then I could easily be content. In my thinking, my contentment depended on other people meeting my needs.

Over the next several months, though, God showed me the real causes of my anger. One of them was my effort to change Larry. I finally realized that my nagging and pouting weren't changing him! I had only one idea left: let God change him. I nervously wondered, "Will God change him to be the husband I need?" Since I seemed to be making the situation even worse, I decided to relinquish control over

Larry's life. This took place at two different levels: in my attitudes and in my actions.

Within my attitudes, I gave up the idea that I could *force* Larry to be what I thought he should be as a Christian, a father, and a husband. I realized that even though my expectations seemed right to me, there was the possibility that my expectations were unrealistic and not really what God expected of Larry. I also came to the conclusion that Larry wasn't responsible for making me happy. Only *I* could make myself happy. The idea that God wanted me to look only to Him for my happiness was a new thought for me. For most of my life I had depended on other people and circumstances for my happiness and contentment. Now God seemed to be telling me, "Regardless of the people and situations around you, look to Me to fill your needs."

In my actions, I stopped verbally condemning Larry for not spending more time with me and the kids. My response was to stop communicating altogether. Even though that wasn't the wisest thing to do, it was what I needed to do to break my old patterns. As time went on, I learned to constructively express myself with "I messages" ("I need to have your complete attention to talk about something") rather than "you messages" ("You never listen to me").

At the beginning, I could keep these new commitments for a short period of time—maybe a few days. Then I would fall back into my old routines—nagging Larry and being disgruntled with life. Suddenly the Spirit's convicting power would remind me of God's new "instructions" for me, and I'd be able to follow them for a slightly longer time. This process of succeeding and failing repeated itself. As several months passed, I realized I was succeeding more often.

Then one day I sensed God's quiet voice within me saying, "Kathy, I want you to tell Larry you love him."

I was shocked. Larry was off flying again and I was

furious that he never included me in any of his plans. "Lord, You know I can't do that. I hate him."

The gentle voice repeated His command. "Kathy, I want you to tell Larry you love him."

"Well, Lord, I certainly will not. I won't be a hypocrite! And besides, if I tell him I love him, he'll think I approve of him being gone so much."

Then the urging seemed to change slightly. "Then I want you to *think* it the next time you see Larry."

I thought that request over and decided to try it. After all, Larry wouldn't hear it and think I was telling him he could continue flying and working long hours.

That day I geared myself up for thinking those three little words—words I hadn't said for at least two years.

Late that afternoon, I heard the garage door go up and the laundry room door open. I hurried down the hall, my heart beating wildly. "I can't do it. . . . You've got to!" My thoughts warred within me.

Larry walked through the laundry room where the pieces of apple still clung to the walls. "Do it now!" a voice screamed within me. I looked Larry straight in the eyes and thought, "I love you. . . ." My mind paused, ". . . but I don't really!"

In that moment, I couldn't even *think* I loved my husband. But as time went on, God softened my heart toward Larry. As I continued to give up trying to force Larry to meet my expectations and chose to find contentment within myself, I became a happier person. Strangely enough, the flame of love for Larry I thought had died began to flicker slightly. Because I didn't focus only on his negative points, I could see a few positives. I remembered why I'd been attracted to him and why I'd married him.

Five months later, God began the healing process in our marriage during a marriage-encounter kind of weekend.

During those forty-four hours, I discovered that Larry still loved me and that I loved him, too. It was a glorious time of recommitting ourselves to our marriage and to each other. But that was only the beginning of learning how to lovingly relate to each other and to communicate effectively.

A month after the weekend, Larry changed jobs. As a result, he took a cut in pay . . . and no longer had the money to fly. Amazed, I saw God working. What I'd been trying to do for several years through nagging and anger, God had accomplished in His timing and in His method. My faith and trust in God's ability to change lives grew as I enjoyed Larry being home more.

Being discontent during troubled relationships is a very natural reaction. Yet God wants to develop within us that supernatural contentment that depends on Him instead of on people or circumstances. It's supernatural because the contentment doesn't come from our old sin nature but from the "new creature" within us that obeys the Spirit.

Although there will be times when contentment is expressed by choosing to act pleasantly around someone even though we aren't happy with him, that doesn't mean we should repress our emotions and never express our disapproval. We can be honest with ourselves and others by facing and sharing those feelings, but at the same time, not allowing them to cause us to react in destructive ways (like screaming, hitting, or name-calling). Being controlled by the Spirit means we control ourselves and express our dissatisfaction in acceptable ways. That involves saying what I want and need and not allowing myself to be abused.

The important thing is to not hang all our hopes for contentment on a relationship—not even our most significant one. I agree with Francois de la Rochefoucauld, who said, "When we cannot find contentment in ourselves it is useless to seek it elsewhere."

An Unsaved Spouse

Samantha is experiencing the heartache that often comes in a marriage between a Christian and a nonChristian. Her husband, Greg, seemed to be a Christian when they were married. Samantha says, "Over the eighteen years of our marriage, Greg has gone from putting up with church to not going at all. Now he goes with me and the children but won't say he's a Christian. In fact, he loves to get me into debates about Christian doctrine. He's a very intelligent man and always wins. I've learned to avoid those discussions.

"During the time Greg didn't go to church, I worried whether he'd turn against me, but my friends encouraged me to keep praying for his salvation. I realized I must study the Word and grow strong in my own faith. That way, when Greg attacks Christianity, I won't weaken in my own trust in God. Even though I've tried to respond wisely to Greg's arguments against Christianity, he hasn't been convinced. When I get frustrated, I write my feelings in my journal or talk with my friends. It doesn't do any good to get angry with Greg. He only uses it as ammunition against the gospel.

"I treasure Acts 16:31: 'Believe in the Lord Jesus, and you shall be saved, you and your household.' I believe that that means my family is set apart and that the counsel coming from my husband—even though he's not a believer—is to be respected. Therefore I consider what he has to say. A wife can make it mighty miserable pulling rank on her husband. I did that for the first five years of our marriage. God had to work hard to pull me out of that.

"My strongest worry that takes away my contentment is Greg's influence on our children. He says that when they're sixteen he's going to tell them all religions are the same. When Greg talks like that, I must trust that God will work it out and that the influence I've had on them will help.

"The other temptation that takes away my contentment

is comparing my family life to other 'perfect' Christian families. I must tell myself that they aren't perfect either."

Samantha has learned many valuable lessons over the
years of coping with an unbelieving spouse.

Wayward Children

Barbara Johnson knows about trusting God for a wayward
child. For eleven years, she prayed for her homosexual son to
be freed from his sinful lifestyle. In the meantime, she
ministered—and continues to minister—to others through
Spatula Ministries and her books, *Where Does a Mother Go to
Resign?* and *Fresh Elastic for Stretched Out Moms.* During
that agonizing time of waiting for God to rescue her son, she
says she learned contentment by "relinquishing my son to
the Lord and refusing to say, 'why me?' I also took heart from
Proverbs 11:21: 'Assuredly, the descendants of the righteous
will be delivered.' I don't consider that a promise but I do
claim it as an encouragement verse.

"When my heart ached, I'd remind myself, 'I've given
this to God.' All we can do is love and pray for our disobe-
dient grown children and give them unconditional love. I
can't change them. The key was to relinquish. God must do it
and He did. I know it doesn't always work out like this, but
my son returned to our home and asked forgiveness. He's a
new person."

Maybe you've been praying for many years for a child
who has turned away from God's principles. Or maybe
you're in the midst of raising your child and even now he's
strong-willed and resistant to your love. Although we have
no guarantees, don't give up praying and disciplining effectively. Parenting is a process that isn't completed with one
great spanking or one deep talk. Contentment will develop as
you accept the fact that your children will never be perfect
and that you are not totally responsible for their actions.

Betty Coble, author of *Women Aware and Choosing* and the director of Women's Ministries at the First Evangelical Free Church in Fullerton, California, explains in her classes that "there is a difference between being responsible to and being responsible for. We are responsible *to* train our children but we are not responsible *for* their decisions."

If you are discontented, it may be that you're thinking you're responsible for your child's decisions. Instead, commit yourself to training and disciplining your child to the best of your ability, and then don't take responsibility for your child's decisions.

Single Parenting

Linda's divorce came five years ago and since then she has been the primary parent for her two daughters, aged six and eight. Her husband divorced her to marry his girlfriend. Linda says, "When Tom first left me, I held on to the fact that God had a plan, that He was in control. Since then, I've gone through cycles of being content and discontented. Right now I'm struggling in discontent because of two main things. First, the struggle with my youngest daughter's severe problems at school, and second, the struggle with relationships with men. I feel like giving up on men because it seems like I keep making poor choices.

"In these difficulties, I haven't gotten to the point of turning them around to trust the Lord completely and thus be content, but I have committed myself to living one day at a time. I'm really trying to allow God to control. In the meantime, I'm being stretched in new areas.

"One of the main reasons I've realized I'm not content is because life isn't going the way I expected. My definition of contentment is knowing life is the way it should be. Because of that, I rely on outward circumstances for my contentment, and I guess I shouldn't because what God is doing isn't always immediately discernible. I'm learning to believe Romans 8:28: God is in control and He'll work everything out for good. Then I experience greater contentment."

Linda is being stretched and "grown" by God as she understands that contentment isn't dependent upon life progressing the way she thinks it should. And how especially important that realization is for a single parent whose life is full of insecurities and tough decisions.

Abusive Past Relationships

When a person has been abused, it's very difficult to find contentment. Barni Feuerhaken knows. She's an incest victim. She says, "When I think of contentment, I think of strength and security. I can be strong and secure knowing 1 Corinthians 10:13 is true. I don't have to struggle about the past because God has not allowed anything in my life that I can't handle in His power. For a person who has been a victim, contentment comes when she knows that she can make choices and that the pain from the past can't control her any longer.

"For me, I've gained control in the relationship between my children and my father. I've told him, 'I don't hate you but I must make sure my children's best interests are protected. From the choices you've made, you don't have their best interests at heart.' He made many promises to my children but didn't keep them, therefore I set the boundaries of their contact with him. Even though he has admitted that the incest occurred, he hasn't changed. I've had to accept that, and that has brought contentment."

Barni has gone through the painful process of working through her pain and rejecting her negative thinking that she must continue as a victim. As a result, she's content with her life, and exhibits strength and security, even ministering to others through a support group she leads.

Like Barni, you too can gain contentment, even if sexual or physical abuse clouds your past.

Friendships

Friendships among women can be a source for either discontent or great contentment. It depends not only on the friend but on our reactions to that friend.

Cindy, a thirty-three-year-old Christian woman, says, "Although I have many good friends, a few seem more harmful than helpful. One of my friends is easily depressed. If I telephone her, she can easily talk for two or three hours. I hesitate to call her and hate myself for my selfishness. When I do try to keep the conversation short, I feel guilty about that. She seems to require more than I have. I know that I love her; it's just that I don't feel very loving at times."

Cindy has made a good point. We may not feel very loving, but we can still choose to love. Saying "I love you" doesn't mean we're lying. It's just that we're not basing our love on our feelings, but on God's unconditional love. In 1 Corinthians 13:4-7 where love is described, it's not listed as a feeling. Instead, it's identified with patience, kindness, lack of jealousy, etc. Those characteristics can be attained by our choice, together with God's strength.

Winkie Pratney, author of several books, defines love as "a choice for the other person's highest good." That definition makes it possible for me to love a person without *feeling* loving. Therefore we don't have to feel guilty. We can feel content in our relationships as we make those loving choices.

A fast way to become discontented is through gossip. Martha knows the sting of gossip. She was leading Stacy, a coworker and new Christian, in a Bible study but found out Stacy was repeating her personal comments to other office workers. She couldn't handle that and ended the study. Then she discovered her adult Sunday school class had gossipers also, so she stopped going there. Discontent with Christians and their fast tongues had defeated her.

As Christians, we often gossip in "acceptable" ways. We'll say, "Oh, we really must pray for Linda. Do you know what she told me?" Or we'll say, "I have a prayer request about Connie. She's in debt to the IRS. We need to pray for her finances." We hide this kind of gossip in robes of "sharing" prayer requests and being "concerned" about people.

But Paul lists gossip in Romans 1:28-30 along with other sins like murder, greed, and hating God. Proverbs 20:19 says, "He who goes about as a slanderer reveals secrets, therefore do not associate with a gossip." Any time we reveal a secret, we are gossiping. A secret is anything we haven't been given permission to tell someone else.

We need to fulfill James 3:2: "If any one does not stumble in what he says, he is a perfect man, able to bridle the whole body."

If you'd like to be more content in your friendships, keep your tongue controlled, refuse to listen to gossip, and only pass along something to someone else after you've received permission from the person it concerns.

Divorce

Divorce has to be one of the most controversial areas in the Christian community right now. Katy knows that. Married for over twenty years, she finally decided to divorce her alcoholic, unfaithful husband. Now that she's made the decision, she's become more content.

"When I think of contentment, I think of calmness in the middle of a hurricane. It's having the assurance that God will get me through this, that He'll guide my steps as I go through this turbulence.

"God strengthened me while I came to a point of making that decision to divorce. For many years I sensed something was wrong but always thought it was my fault. Then I finally faced the reality that my husband was responsible too, and realized I had to take another approach. Through extensive counseling and confronting him with his alcoholism in an intervention, I began to see through the thick fog and trust God to make some needed changes.

"I'm still scared to death, wondering if I've made a mistake, wondering if God can bless me. But by noticing how God has guided me so far, I've gained a measure of contentment and confidence that He will continue to do that. It's possible to be content in spite of struggles because God's peace is stronger than my troubles. That doesn't mean I'll always feel bubbly, but I can rest knowing He'll never leave me or forsake me."

Paul and Barnabas

Relationships in the early Church weren't always perfect, just as they aren't perfect now. Even Christians like Paul and Barnabas had problems in this area.

In Acts 15:36-40, we see disagreement between these two great Christians. Paul didn't want to take John Mark on their next missionary journey because Mark had abandoned them during an earlier trip. Barnabas believed John Mark had matured and wanted him to come.

Their disagreement became so sharp that "they separated from one another, and Barnabas took Mark with him and sailed away to Cyprus. But Paul chose Silas and departed" (verses 39-40). Even though this disagreement wasn't a very good example for others, we can see how God used it, for now two teams of missionaries went out instead of one. And of course, we know that these discontented relationships were healed later. Paul instructed Timothy in 2 Timothy 4:11, "Pick up Mark and bring him with you, for he is useful to me for service."

God's Love

It is love, God's very nature, on which we must concentrate to develop contentment in our relationships. Paul's prayer for the Ephesians shows God's desire for us: "And I pray that you, being rooted and established in love, may have power, together with all the saints, to grasp how wide and long and high and deep is the love of Christ, and to know this love that surpasses knowledge—that you may be filled to the measure of all the fullness of God" (Ephesians 3:17-19, NIV).

As we grow to fully understand how much God loves us, we are more able to love others because God's love is sufficient to make us content. We don't have to claw and grasp from others what only God can provide.

Yet while we're traveling toward that level of contentment, we do need guidelines for dealing with those troubled relationships that may be diluting our contentment. Here are some principles to consider:

1. *We can't save or control anyone else.* Psalm 49:7 tells us, "No man can by any means redeem his brother, or give to God a ransom for him." If our discontent stems from our relationship with an unbeliever, we can become more content by releasing the responsibility for saving that person. Of course, we should commit to being the best wife, mother, relative, or friend we can be. But thinking that we must be perfect so that this person will come to know the Lord can take away our contentment. Instead, we can release that person to God's convicting power.

It's the same when we find ourselves thinking that we should control others—to make them do what we think is best. Obviously, we have a responsibility to discipline a child to encourage him to obey us, but when dealing with an adult—whether a grown child, a husband, a relative, or a friend—we don't have that same responsibility. We can try to influence someone by communicating appropriately, but ultimately we cannot change another person.

Yes, there may be a need to take some kind of action, like an intervention confrontation with an alcoholic or removing ourselves from an abusive person, but we'll only become discontent if we think it's our responsibility to make the other person change.

Contentment will be strengthened when we release that difficult person to God's control and become solely responsible for changing ourselves to be who God wants us to be.

2. *No one else is a reflection of us.* We may be discontented because we think someone else's actions define who we are. That's not true. His choices only demonstrate who he is.

Dr. Larry Crabb, Christian psychologist, says a mother must "change her thinking from 'I need my child to turn out right if I am to be worthwhile' to 'I am worthwhile as a responsible child of God. I do, of course, want my child to turn out right so I will discipline him in what I understand to be a biblical manner. If my child responds poorly, I will be grieved and will reevaluate my discipline procedures to make sure they are biblical, but I will not be personally threatened because my needs are not at stake. They do not depend on my child's response.'"[1]

We can be content by understanding that our husband, child, and friend are representing themselves—not us.

3. *Comparisons are a dead end.* No person is perfect and no relationship is perfect. But the enemy wants us to think that others are perfect so that we'll become discouraged. Unfortunately, not many Christians reveal their inadequacies and failures. Most are trying to keep their masks of Super Christian and Super Mom intact. As a result, we think we're the only ones who scream at our kids or get upset with our husbands.

We can be content knowing that we're not the only ones struggling in a relationship. We can also grow in contentment by realizing that even if our beloved unbeliever comes to know the Lord, he or she *still* won't be perfect. New believers will still have many of the same personality flaws and inadequacies they had as unbelievers.

4. *Withdrawing love is never the answer.* Many of us believe we can't be content and joyful because then that uncooperative person will think he doesn't have to change. We think withdrawing love will make that person change. But it doesn't work that way.

Rich Buhler in his book *Love: No Strings Attached* identifies how Jesus gave unconditional love. "The Pharisees, the religious leaders of Jesus' day, advocated total separation from the people who most needed to hear their message, particularly prostitutes and tax collectors. Jesus did not condone prostitution or any other kind of promiscuity; neither did He approve of the tax collectors' apparent fraud and greed. However, He befriended these people, ate with them (which was a direct violation of pharisaical law), showed them His love, and won their commitment to His message, a message which required them to change their ways."[2]

Like Jesus, we need to offer unconditional love while expressing our disapproval in gentle words. That means that we still take joy in our husband's sexual advances, even if he doesn't do all the chores. That we still listen to our husband's counsel, even if he isn't a Christian. That we still have a smile for a friend who hasn't forgiven us. That we still welcome our young adult into our home, even though he or she is promiscuous. In each of these situations, we can tell the other person what displeases us, but we should not withdraw our love.

There may be occasions, though, when we must withdraw our physical presence if we're being abused. A woman should get professional help and not allow herself to be beaten by an alcoholic husband or allow a child to be sexually molested. In these cases, the most loving action is to contact the police or authorities so that the other person will get the help he needs. If a husband is making wrong choices because he's using cocaine, the wife may choose to control their income and confront him with his addiction. But even in these painful situations, we can continue to move toward greater contentment because we know that the God who lives in us is greater than any problem we're facing.

Becoming content in relationships is likely one of the most effective ways God continues the learning process within us. But we *can* experience success.

Just recently I saw how much I've grown in my ability to share my needs and thus stay content. When Larry expressed his desire to make a major purchase that seemed to primarily benefit him, I reacted in an acceptable way. In the old days, I would have attacked him out of insecurity and fear by saying something like, "That's just like you. You think only of yourself, never of my needs." But this time, I said, "I can understand why you want to buy that, but I've mentioned several times how I've wanted something else and you didn't want to spend the money." I was in tears because of the intensity of my feelings and I allowed my emotions to show. But I didn't allow my frustration and anger to make me react destructively. Larry and I talked for a long time about each of our desires and we came to an acceptable compromise. What a difference from many years ago!

Now that Larry and I are looking forward to our eighteenth wedding anniversary, I can say it is possible to achieve contentment. I *am* content to be where I am now: married to Larry and mothering two children.

NOTES: 1. Larry J. Crabb, Jr., *Effective Biblical Counseling,* page 140, used by permission.
2. Rich Buhler, *Love: No Strings Attached* (Nashville: Thomas Nelson Inc., Publishers, 1987), page 35, used by permission.

8
Contentment During Physical Affliction

I'm a baby when it comes to pain. Although the only times I've been in the hospital have been for my own birth and to give birth to two children, I have occupied the dentist's chair more times than I'd like to remember. Larry teases me by saying if he'd known my genes made such bad teeth, he never would have married me. I sometimes quip that after I die, he can melt me down, get all the gold from my crowns and be rich.

Because my teeth are so weak, I often experience pain. And when I'm in pain, everyone better watch out. I'm grumpy. After the dentist fixes me up, I regret that I couldn't have been more patient. I tell myself I'll do better the next time, but I'm not much improved then either.

So it comes as a great surprise to me that there are people who are content even in the midst of pain and physical handicaps. I wonder how they do it.

Tom and Ginny

Tom and Ginny Carr shared their secrets with me. They both experience physical handicaps that hamper their mobility and create pain within their bodies. Yet they are happily married and content.

Tom has multiple sclerosis and is confined to a wheelchair. Formerly employed as a nuclear/environmental engineer, he is a fun-loving man with a wonderful sense of humor. As a result, he makes other people feel comfortable. Before his illness was diagnosed and he came to know the Lord, he had hoped to be a professional tennis player.

Whereas Tom has faced his handicap for only about seventeen years, his petite and vivacious wife, Ginny, has coped with her handicap since childhood. She contracted polio at age two-and-a-half. But walking with a leg brace and crutches didn't stop her from being voted high school homecoming queen and exuding God's love now through her beautiful smile and skillful flute playing.

Tom says, "Contentment is accepting the way things are when you can't change them. I go along with Paul in Philippians 4:11 that 'I have learned to be content in my circumstances.'

"I think unrealistic expectations take away contentment. It gets easier to be content with realistic expectations. There are days, of course, when my situation is discouraging because I can't do something I'd like, but I've learned to accept and live within my limitations."

It isn't long into the conversation before Tom is talking about his favorite subject, his wonderful wife. "I know that

I'm married to the world's greatest woman. I am absolutely content with Ginny. She may not look like Cheryl Tiegs, but she is very beautiful and courageous. She has taken what she has and developed it to the fullest potential. It's hard for Ginny to cook really fancy meals, but among the issues of life, that's trivial. Ginny's unconditional love and acceptance of me is far more important than any specific thing she does.

"We honestly don't have fights. Since the day we met, we've made praying together a first priority. Even if I'm out of town, we pray together by phone. That's the source of our contentment: our commitment to the Lord bonds us to each other.

"Dealing with the big issues also bonds us together. When I fall out of bed onto the floor and can't get up by myself, I realize how much I need Ginny. In the six years, four months, and one day we've been married, we've discovered that the difference between contentment and conflict is the ability to laugh—even when I'm on the floor.

"I'm thankful for my handicap because it's given me the opportunity to live life with more depth. It took me from living a fast and easy lifestyle to being in touch with God. When I graduated from college, I was convinced I'd become President of the United States. My handicap humbled me— I realized I couldn't do those great things, that first I needed God. Then I came to know the Lord and thought He would heal me. It wasn't until I recognized Ginny as more than a friend, but as my future bride, that I could hear God say, 'Tom, your healing is in Ginny.'

"If I'd been physically healed, I'd never be as well as I am now being afflicted to the point of humility. Contentment is letting God reign and rule in your life."

Ginny adds, "Contentment is accepting and being thankful. My hardest area to be content in is my limited energy level. I have to take it slow and ask, 'Am I uniquely suited to do this particular thing?' It's frustrating not to be able to do all the things I'd like.

"Tom and I see perfectly healthy couples getting upset about little things. With our handicaps, we have bigger issues that must be dealt with. Once they're taken care of, we usually don't have enough energy to get uptight about the little things.

"Tom always raises my self-esteem by focusing on what I can do, rather than on what I can't do. God in His mercy allowed me to have this handicap because He uses it to make me the person He wants me to be. Without my handicap, I'd be a totally different person. And since I tend to be strong-willed and determined, God allowed the handicap to bring those characteristics into line. My life with polio is richer than if I'd never had it."

Tom and Ginny have discovered the secret of being content: trusting God to show them the important things in life.

If we noticed little pleasures,
As we notice little pains—
If we quite forgot our losses
And remembered all our gains.

If we looked for people's virtues
And their faults refused to see.
What a comfortable, happy, cheerful place
This world would be![1]

Judy
Judy is another person who has persevered in life and marriage in spite of multiple sclerosis and difficulties. Judy was diagnosed with the disease in 1984, after suffering from its symptoms for several years. She is confined to bed except for

the times she's in her wheelchair. Her husband was laid off from work shortly after her diagnosis and has been developing new skills in a different occupation. With two grown daughters and a teenage son, she has had to depend on other people to a great extent and ultimately upon God.

"One source of my discontent," Judy says, "is low self-esteem because I can't contribute much. But even then God is faithful. I recently read in our church's newsletter that they needed someone to make phone calls for the Food Fund, a program that gives donated food to needy families. At first I thought, 'They wouldn't want me.' But after I saw the announcement for the second week I phoned and found out no one else had called. I've been doing it ever since and it builds my self-esteem. People say I take the time to talk to them. I'm glad the Lord has given me two ministries: calling for the Food Fund and praying for people. It makes me feel more content. I feel like I'm doing more than just lying here.

"My recipe for contentment is don't think of yourself all the time. That was a problem with me. Instead, find something to do so you don't dwell on yourself. That has helped me a lot."

Judy has discovered another secret for contentment in the midst of pain and handicap: think of others.

Robert

I couldn't tell from looking at sixty-year-old Robert Yocum's tall, energetic frame and broad smile that he suffered from a fatal illness. He has a severe form of lupus, causing an inflammation of the connective tissues.

Robert says, "Before the doctors could pinpoint what had taken away my strength and endurance, I felt trapped and caged. Fear, anger, and impatience took their toll on me. When I found out I had lupus, I wondered, 'How am I going to cope with this? Will I ever live a normal life again?' None of my doctors knew. I was told there was no known cure, and life expectancy was five years.

"The challenge to prove I could live longer than five years entered my mind and my attitude changed dramatically. I read from the Bible constantly and found strength and hope from the book of Job. I decided, 'This is a new experience for me and I don't know how it's going to turn out. Since I must live with this illness the rest of my life, why don't I turn it into an adventure?'

"That adventure included finding new approaches to life because my body could no longer keep up with me. I said to myself, 'I'm not a victim. I'm a free person and have the freedom to live my life within this new set of circumstances.'

"Another thought that has been a great help to me is from Jeremiah 18: the potter working at his wheel. I have pictured myself being turned on the wheel of circumstances, and God, with His tender hands, is shaping me into the vessel He wants me to be.

"Contentment comes through the hard experiences that confront us in life as we surrender our will to the will of God. Rather than fretting about my illness, or feeling I was experiencing a great misfortune in life, I accepted the illness as a part of life and turned it into an adventure."

Robert has succeeded in his adventure. Not only has he lived longer than five years, but he has allowed God to use his illness for good by writing about it and helping others.

Tim

Tim Hansel is no exception. The author of *You Gotta Keep Dancin'*, Tim injured his back during a mountain climbing accident in 1974.

He gives this account in his book, "I can't remember when I last woke up feeling good. Each morning continues another layer of nauseating pain, stiffness, the dull gray ache, and the never-ending fatigue.

"I chose to accept the pain as aggressively as possible. I continued my work with Summit Expedition, a wilderness/mountaineering ministry which Pam and I had started in 1970. I kept on climbing, jogging, and playing tennis . . ." until he tore several ribs from his spine and the pain increased.

"My emotions were like a Duncan yo-yo. I discovered real depression firsthand. I had no idea how to anticipate the pain or cope with it. Perhaps I was going through the stages identified by Kubler-Ross in relation to death and dying. These stages apply to any kind of loss, that of a loved one or of a part of oneself.

"The first stage is *denial*—not believing that it's really happening. The second stage is *bargaining,* trying to equivocate with God to make deals. The third stage is *anger,* the rage that comes from within based upon frustration which cannot be satiated. The fourth stage is *depression,* a symptom of both prolonged anger turned inward and guilt. The final stage is *acceptance,* realizing that what is, is—and is going to be.

"I had a choice. I knew by [then] that the damage was permanent . . . and that pain would be a companion for the rest of my journey. I had to learn a whole new way of living or fold up my cards.

"Slowly my rage to live emerged from the depression, frustration, and anger. But when it was there I realized that it had a taste to it that I'd never known before. I began to see life in a way that never would have been possible before. I began to relish small, daily, simple things—and realized at a depth that never seemed possible that *all* of life was sacred. There were moments, though sporadic and far apart, when I began to understand that life wasn't over for me—but perhaps was just beginning.

"Some time later . . . I discovered Nehemiah 8:10, 'The joy of the Lord is *your strength.*' . . . I had without knowing or intending it, put a lid on [life] by saying to myself, 'When I am strong, then I'll be joyful. When the pain eases, then I'll be joyful.'

"The problem was reality. The pain didn't subside. And I had placed myself in the position of waiting until things got better, waiting until I knew more of God, waiting until I had enough strength to be joyful. But through this profound and simple passage from Nehemiah, God reminded me again and again that I cannot choose to be strong, but I can choose to be joyful. And when I am willing to do that, strength will follow."[2]

Tim Hansel has discovered how to live above his circumstances, even when the circumstances include a constant dull, gray ache of pain.

H.A. Ironside said, "Christ is enough to satisfy the hearts of all who confide in Him and who leave everything in His hands. Such need never be cast down by seeming misfortunes.

"A Christian asked another how he was getting along. Dolefully his friend replied, 'Oh, fairly well, under the circumstances.'

"'I am sorry,' exclaimed the other, 'that you are under the circumstances. The Lord would have us living above all circumstances, where He Himself can satisfy our hearts and meet our every need for time and eternity.'"

Eileen

"I am the daughter whose presence on the delivery table would have devastated most mothers," says Eileen Cronin Noe.

"Imagine the scenario: 'Mrs. Smith,' the doctor says, 'you have a baby girl.'

"'Is she pretty?' Mrs. Smith asks. 'Can I hold her?'

"The doctor stammers, 'Mrs. Smith, your baby is missing most of her legs.'

"The doctor gives the mother a tiny infant whose right leg is missing from a point just above the place where a knee might have been and whose left leg has a knee with only a small, underdeveloped portion of a lower calf extending from it.

"This is what my body resembled at birth—and still does. The agent that caused this was most likely thalidomide. For my parents, abortion was not an option, even had they been aware of my condition. They believe that it was God's decision, and they were content with that decision. Their belief has led me to accept—even prefer—things for what they are.

"What I feel I needed to hear again and again in my childhood is something like, 'You're different. We're not sure why. There isn't anything we can do about it. We love you very much, and we're glad that you're here.'

"To help me lead a normal life, my parents taught me never to underestimate my capabilities. Being different was an idea that never did quite settle into my mind. Yet, just as I began to believe that I had conquered this thing called disability, I learned that it was not a thing to be conquered. Rather, it was something to accept.

"When [my husband, Paul, and I] have children, our chances of having a disabled child are probably no greater than most people's.

"As far as the emotional side of [having a child] is concerned, I will have to deal realistically with a child who might at times feel embarrassed by my physical differences.

"It will be difficult, but I have learned to understand others' discomfort and curiosity about my differences. Most importantly, I look forward to teaching my child to love himself or herself in ways that most children will never have a chance to learn."[3]

Eileen has expressed a beautiful attitude about her handicap, an attitude of joy and contentment.

The Apostle Paul

A chapter on physical affliction wouldn't be complete without including the experience of the apostle Paul. In 2 Corinthians 11:23-27, it takes five verses to list all the painful things he went through: lashings, beatings, stonings, shipwreck, physical dangers, robbers, sleeplessness, hunger, thirst, cold, and exposure. And he also carried the emotional pain of caring for the churches.

The next chapter tells us he suffered from a physical illness. Many theologians believe it was some eye deformity or disease. So Paul knew what it was like to be in pain and to have a part of his body not work perfectly. Yet *contentment* is a word he used often in his writings. Here are some from the many passages:

"There was given me a thorn in the flesh, a messenger of Satan to buffet me—to keep me from exalting myself! Concerning this I entreated the Lord three times that it might depart from me. And He has said to me, 'My grace is sufficient for you, for power is perfected in weakness.' Most gladly, therefore, I will rather boast about my weaknesses, that the power of Christ may dwell in me. Therefore I am well content with weaknesses, with insults, with distresses, with persecutions, with difficulties, for Christ's sake; for when I am weak, then I am strong" (2 Corinthians 12:7-10).

"Not that I speak from want; for I have learned to be content in whatever circumstances I am. I know how to get along with humble means, and I also know how to live in prosperity; in any and every circumstance I have learned the secret of being filled and going hungry, both of having abundance and suffering need" (Philippians 4:11-12).

"But godliness actually is a means of great gain, when accompanied by contentment. For we have brought nothing into the world, so we cannot take anything out of it either. And if we have food and covering, with these we shall be content" (1 Timothy 6:6-8).

If Paul with his many difficulties could choose and learn contentment, then there is certainly hope for you and me.

God's Mercy

When we think of physical affliction, we may wonder which characteristic of God will help us the most to be content. I believe it's His mercy. Mercy can be defined as "to feel sympathy with the misery of another, and especially sympathy manifested in act."[4]

As the Greek noun *eleos*, it means "the outward manifestation of pity; it assumes need on the part of him who receives it and resources adequate to meet the need on the part of him who shows it."[5] I like that definition because it reminds me that God does have adequate resources to meet the needs of a person in physical affliction and to give him contentment.

W.E. Vine says, "Mercy is the act of God, peace is the resulting experience in the heart of man. Grace describes God's attitude toward the law-breaker and the rebel; mercy is His attitude toward those who are in distress."[6]

If anyone is in distress, it's the person who experiences pain and handicap, especially when he or she has prayed for a long time to be healed. This is where discontent can have its deepest hold in a person's life. The thinking of a person seeking a healing may be something like this: "I've prayed to be healed and I'm desperate. I can't live with this any longer. I must be healed or die. I must develop more faith so that God will heal me."

That kind of thinking wipes out contentment. What should our attitude be? I think it can best be summed up by Tim Hansel when he writes, "For years, people have asked me, 'Haven't you prayed to the Lord for healing?'

"My obvious answer: 'Of course.'

"'Why do you think he hasn't healed you?'

"'He has.'

"'But I thought you were still in pain.'

"'I am.'

"'I don't understand.'

"'I have prayed hundreds, if not thousands, of times for the Lord to heal me—and he finally *healed me of the need to be healed.*' I had discovered a peace inside the pain.

"I finally came to the realization that if the Lord could use this body better the way it is, then that's the way it should be. I'm quite sure that I would be a different person, were it not for my accident."[7]

Contentment is the result of praying for healing, believing that God's mercy is sympathetic with my pain, and trusting God to give the right answer, whether it's "no," "yes," or "wait." The final ingredient is acceptance of that answer. That acceptance has space for continuing to ask for a healing, but at the same time, there's an accompanying peace that means, "I'll accept whatever God decides."

From Paul's writings about contentment, we can make these final conclusions:

We can be content while in physical affliction because God will make the correct decision regarding our condition.

We can be content while in physical affliction because weaknesses force us to be strong in Christ.

We can be content while in physical affliction because contentment is something we can learn.

We can be content while in physical affliction because we were never guaranteed we'd be free from pain in this life.

I'm going to remember Paul's exhortations, along with the example of Tim, Eileen, Judy, Robert, Tom, and Ginny, the next time I have a toothache. And if that doesn't work, I'll remind myself of the ninety-seven-year-old man I read about in the newspaper. He's had the hiccups for over fifty years and has tried hundreds of remedies—to no avail. He says he's grown content and can live with them, but is willing to try anything if it'll give him an uninterrupted night's sleep.

I'd rather have a toothache.

NOTES: 1. *Forbes Magazine of Business,* quoted in *Great Quotes and Illustrations,* George Sweeting, ed. (Waco, Tex.: Word, Inc., 1985), page 71.

2. Tim Hansel, *You Gotta Keep Dancin'* (Elgin, Ill.: David C. Cook Publishing Company, 1985), pages 15,35,37,47, used by permission.

3. Eileen Cronin Noe, "Being Different: A Personal Story of Thalidomide," *Los Angeles Times* (July 22, 1987), Part V, pages 1,3.

4. W.E. Vine, *Vine's Expository Dictionary of Old and New Testament Words* (Old Tappan, N.J.: Fleming H. Revell, 1981), page 61.

5. Vine, *Expository Dictionary,* page 60.

6. Vine, *Expository Dictionary,* page 61.

7. Hansel, *You Gotta Keep Dancin',* pages 123-124, used by permission.

9
Contentment During Success

Things had been going smoothly for too long. It just didn't feel right. Oh, sure, there were the little things of life that were irritating and frustrating, but no "biggies"—not the kind of monumental incidents other people were experiencing. I felt doomed before the inevitable, as if it were just a matter of time before something bad—I mean really bad—would happen. Like the calm before the storm, the ease of my life made me wonder when the clouds would blow in the rain.

Time went on and still nothing big crashed onto the scene. Oh, Mark did have an asthma attack for the first time at age nine. His medicine changed his personality from a nice little boy to a terrorist. If we hadn't found a medication that worked without changing his personality, this might have qualified as that ominous storm. But after several months, Mark was able to go off the medicine completely and take care of any little attacks with asthma spray.

So this incident didn't quite seem like the "biggie" I was anticipating. Surely there had to be something more devastating that would arrive any moment. After all, God prunes and purges through testing, right? He certainly couldn't let me off the hook of testing for too long, or else I wouldn't grow spiritually.

Thinking this way made it seem as if God were holding an ax labeled "testing" over my spiritual head waiting for just the right moment to let it fall and clobber me. I continued my holding pattern of "when will it fall?"

Several months passed and *still nothing big.* I couldn't believe it. This couldn't be God's way of working! I became more paranoid. The longer I waited, the larger the expected "biggie" grew in my mind. I was convinced that God would have the ax fall down on me in a major way very soon. I thought about it constantly. "When is it going to happen?" The sense of a coming disaster shoved contentment right out of my life.

Several months passed and still nothing big! Then it dawned on me. "I'm not being very content with success, am I? I'm paranoid that something bad is going to happen and I'm not even enjoying this time of calm God has graciously given me. I'm pretty stupid not to just thank God for this blessing and trust that if something does happen later, He'll strengthen me to deal with it. Why wish disaster upon yourself, Kathy? Wise up!"

Little by little, over the following months, the image of that ax slowly disappeared from my thinking as I chose to thank God for the absence of great trials.

That's what I'd like to examine in this chapter—how to

learn contentment during success. By "success" I mean the absence of major trials and the presence of some level of prosperity.

Martie

Martie, a thirty-six-year-old woman who's been a Christian for three years, has had feelings similar to mine. For the past year, she and her husband have experienced financial and personal success. This came after their first business failed, putting them $20,000 in debt. Now God has abundantly blessed them and yet Martie can't seem to get a firm grasp on contentment.

"I don't feel content because after having things be stressful for so long, I can't believe this success will last. I'm afraid anything I do wrong will snap me back into the trials like before. There seems to be a connection in my thinking between me doing things wrong and then my circumstances becoming disastrous.

"I relied on the Lord very heavily during the times of debt and struggle. It seemed like He was the only one who could help me. Even though I was a new Christian, I figured I had no choice.

"Now that God in His goodness has brought the prosperous circumstances I prayed for, I can't be content because I'm afraid if I'm less than perfect, He'll zap me. If I don't pray or read the Bible, I'm afraid something will happen to me the next day. I don't really think that's how God works, so I must correct my thinking. But I do think God is asking me, 'Are you going to depend upon Me when you don't need to financially or emotionally?'

"Before, I memorized Scripture faithfully, and even generously gave from our little bit of income with no expectation of reward—even though we were in great debt. I relied on Luke 12:31 daily: 'He will always give you all you need from day to day if you will make the Kingdom of God your primary concern' (TLB).

"Now I try to memorize Scripture, but it doesn't seem to have as much meaning. And even though we have an abundance of money, I find it difficult to give our tithe. This is crazy. When my situation was stressful, it was easy to trust Him, but now that my circumstances are fairly smooth, it's more difficult. I thought it would be the opposite. Now it's a difficult choice for me to trust God and I think He must be displeased with me."

I reassured Martie that actually God was very pleased with her because she was choosing to trust Him even though her circumstances didn't require it to a large measure. God had given her a special grace during that time of trial, which empowered her to be strong in Him, especially since she had only known Him a short time. Now that she'd grown in her Christian life and was financially prosperous, turning to Him when she didn't have to meant she was making wise choices—and that pleased Him.

Martie is learning to be content even during success by rejecting her fear, and trusting God instead. Eventually, contentment will be fruitful in her life.

Alicia

Alicia is pregnant with her second child and her life is fairly trial-free, even though it's not perfect. She says, "Right now Craig and I certainly are not well-off, but we're not in debt either, like we used to be. I'd like to own a house instead of living in an apartment, but I am content, even if I don't want to be living here forever. It's true I'd like some things to be different, but if they were, I wouldn't be any more content.

"I would like my relationship with Craig to improve and for him to become a Christian, but even then I wouldn't be more content. I feel confident with God. I depend upon what

I call my 'major prayer' with God each day, but if I don't pray, I don't feel like I have to earn back His grace.

"To me, contentment is relief from pressure. God has graciously been working things out in my life recently and I've grown to trust that He'll do that in everything. Therefore I don't have to feel pressured.

"For instance, last month I wasn't needed at my part-time job for three weeks, so we didn't have that money coming in. It turned out that Craig went out of town for his job and had to work 103 hours while there. So he got paid more than double his usual salary and that made up for my lack of work. That's why I don't get discontented about things: I know God will provide.

"Of course, there was a time in my life when I was very discontented. Craig was unfaithful and I had to make a decision. Because he didn't want out of the marriage, I decided to make a commitment to stick it out. I care more about my relationship with God than what the world says about divorce.

"I still don't feel completely loving toward Craig. When he was away, I didn't miss him. I started thinking how easy it would be to live without him. Then I realized that my negative thinking could make me act in a way I might regret, so I consciously chose to think God's way. My prayer and hope is that Craig and I will someday share a Christian marriage."

One of the main reasons Alicia experiences contentment during success is because she has learned to take "every thought captive to the obedience of Christ" (2 Corinthians 10:5). When she begins to think negatively, she turns her thoughts back to God's way of thinking and that restores her contentment.

A secondary cause of Alicia's contentment is her decision to make a commitment to her marriage. Dr. James Dobson says about commitment, "What will you do, then, when unexpected tornadoes blow through your home, or when the doldrums leave your sails sagging and silent? Will you pack it in and go home to mama? Will you pout and cry and seek ways to strike back? Or will your commitment hold you steady?

"These questions must be addressed *now*, before Satan has an opportunity to put his noose of discouragement around your neck. Set your jaw and clench your fists. Nothing short of death must ever be permitted to come between the two of you. *Nothing!*"[1]

This principle applies to anything we're involved in. If I'm committed to completing a task or loving a person or reaching a goal, I'll be more determined to finish this pursuit even if obstacles block my way. As a result, my mind won't be tossed back and forth by indecision. I'll be more content.

Dangers of Success

When success arrives and seems to be staying around awhile, there are several dangers we must guard against.

The first is *pride*. Pride results when I view my success and think, "Yep, that's just like me to bring success into my life. I sure do deserve this time of prosperity." Pride credits my efforts for the success. In reality, it's God's gift, although I have been a partner in His plan by making wise choices.

The second danger is *selfishness*. If I don't choose contentment, my success will make me focus on myself to the extent that I won't respond to the needs of others. Instead of using this valuable time as an opportunity of reaching out to others to an even greater degree, I'll concentrate only on my good fortune.

Closely related to selfishness is the third danger: *greed*. As I'm concentrating on my own good fortune, I may want to keep my prosperity clutched in my own hot fists. Now that I've gotten what I'd like—prosperity—I'm suddenly terrified it'll slip from my grasp. I hold on to it even more tightly and don't want to share it with others.

The final danger of success is *self-sufficiency*. It's the attitude that I've earned this present condition and it's up to me to keep the good things coming. No longer am I content with God's provision. I'm worried because I must provide for my own needs.

The result of this downward spiral is discontent. My eyes are off the Lord and on myself. That very thing happened to King Uzziah.

In 2 Chronicles 26, we read about Uzziah, who became king of Judah at the age of sixteen and ruled for fifty-two years. He started out doing what was right in God's eyes and "as long as he sought the LORD, God prospered him" (2 Chronicles 26:5). That prosperity included being victorious in wars, enjoying wealth, building many cities, having fertile fields, and being famous among many nations.

Then in 2 Chronicles 26:16, we read about Uzziah's change of heart. "But when he became strong, his heart was so proud that he acted corruptly, and he was unfaithful to the LORD his God, for he entered the temple of the LORD to burn incense on the altar of incense." Uzziah's pride and self-sufficiency made him think he could disobey God's rule that only a priest should offer incense in the Temple. When confronted with his sin, he got angry. God struck him with leprosy, and his son Jotham ruled in his place.

Uzziah fell to the temptations of success. He credited himself, not God, for his prosperity and victories. We can be tempted to think the same way. What is the solution to these dangers? Let's look at King Solomon for some answers.

Solomon

Of all the people in the history of mankind, King Solomon experienced the greatest success and prosperity. God gave him both tremendous wisdom and excessive material wealth.

His book—Ecclesiastes—tells how Solomon dealt with the vanity of his accomplishments and thus gained contentment. At his lowest point he lamented, "So I hated life, for the work which had been done under the sun was grievous to me; because everything is futility and striving after wind. Thus I hated all the fruit of my labor for which I had labored under the sun, for I must leave it to the man who will come after me" (Ecclesiastes 2:17-18).

Yet he eventually came to a point of contentment where he said, "There is nothing better for a man than to eat and drink and tell himself that his labor is good. This also I have seen, that it is from the hand of God" (Ecclesiastes 2:24).

Let's take a look at a smattering of verses from Ecclesiastes to discover principles for contentment during success.

1. *The contented woman understands that success may bring fickle popularity.* "A poor, yet wise lad is better than an old and foolish king who no longer knows how to receive instruction. For he has come out of prison to become king, even though he was born poor in his kingdom. I have seen *all the living under the sun throng to the side of the second lad* who replaces him. There is no end to all the people, to all who were before them, and *even the ones who will come later will not be happy with him,* for this too is vanity and striving after wind" (Ecclesiastes 4:13-16, italics added).

This somewhat confusing passage tells us that even popularity doesn't bring contentment. Even after a person becomes king, there will still be people who are unhappy with him, though they initially thronged to his side.

That happened in my own attitudes as a friend of mine rose to the leadership of an organization. Suddenly, she was no longer "one of us," but "one of them." It became easy to criticize her and misunderstand her motives, even though she continued to act the same loving way she had before.

I had to remind myself that she was the same person; she'd just been put in a different position.

It's true that success can often bring new and adoring people into our lives, but we mustn't depend upon them for our contentment. That popularity is temporary.

2. *The contented woman understands that success isn't the advantage it might seem.* "He who loves money will not be satisfied with money, nor he who loves abundance with its income. This too is vanity. When good things increase, those who consume them increase. So what is the advantage to their owners except to look on? The sleep of the working man is pleasant, whether he eats little or much. But the full stomach of the rich man does not allow him to sleep" (Ecclesiastes 5:10-12).

When a woman is beset by trials or poverty, she may think, "When I get over these trials and get some money in the bank, I'll have all my problems solved." That kind of thinking will only set up attitudes of discontent when success and prosperity arrive, for wealth has its own problems. She'll find out that she still has problems and that contentment is just as elusive as before.

Therefore, the woman who is content doesn't expect success to wipe away problems. Instead, she depends on God to help her deal with her problems regardless of which kinds they are.

3. *The contented woman understands that success isn't the goal; it's a means to an end.* "As he had come naked from his mother's womb, so will he return as he came. He will take nothing from the fruit of his labor that he can carry in his hand" (Ecclesiastes 5:15).

Robert G. Lee points out, "Writer Bert Bacharach tells us that the highest income made in a year was Al Capone's 'take' in 1927—reputed to have been one hundred and five *million* dollars. But his *'take'* when he died was nothing—

zero. No money was in his shroud—his hands were empty—even as the hands of all the poor and all the rich are empty when burial is accomplished."

Life, along with its accompanying success and prosperity, is not the goal. It's only a means to the end: eternity. If I don't maintain this attitude, though, I can quickly become discontented when success arrives and I think, "Is that all there is? I thought life at the top would be wonderful." No, it's making righteous choices with God's help, not arriving at what the world calls success. In fact, we may find as Dr. Howard Hendricks, professor at Dallas Theological Seminary, says, "When you play the game of climbing the ladder to success, you may reach the top and find that, all the time, the ladder was resting against the wrong wall."[2]

Realizing that success or wealth is not the goal will help us stay tuned to what God considers success. As Charles Malik says, "Success is neither fame, wealth nor power; rather it is seeking, knowing, loving and obeying God. If you seek, you will know; if you know, you will love; if you love, you will obey."

4. *The contented woman understands that today's success should not be compared with the past.* "Do not say, 'Why is it that the former days were better than these?' For it is not from wisdom that you ask about this" (Ecclesiastes 7:10).

Even though we know we had trials and pain in former days, it's easy to forget the anguish and instead glorify the past. It's like childbirth. As I experienced the pain of labor, I vowed I'd never do it again. But as soon as I saw the result—that beautiful child—I quickly forgot the pain and looked forward to having another child.

The same thing can happen when we're in a period of rest from trials. Seeing now the good changes in our lives, we can almost (I said "almost"!) begin to yearn for new trials. Such an attitude only makes us discontented with our pres-

ent successful circumstances—which are a gift from God.
Instead, we must not compare today with yesterday or yesterday with today. God will work out His special plan that is
individual and unique for each day.

5. *The contented woman understands that success is a gift
from God, not something she has earned.* "In the day of
prosperity be happy, but in the day of adversity consider—
God has made the one as well as the other so that man may
not discover anything that will be after him" (Ecclesiastes
7:14).

As soon as we begin to take credit for the blessings we've
received, we're doomed to discontent because we've put our
faith in ourselves. Instead, we should consider ourselves as
"a turtle on a fence post." That phrase was evidently coined
by Dr. Robert Lamont while pastoring the First Presbyter-
ian Church in Pittsburgh, Pennsylvania. He said, "When I
was a schoolboy we would occasionally see a turtle on a fence
post, and when we did we knew someone had put him there.
He didn't get there by himself. That is how I see my own life.
I'm a turtle on a fence post."[3]

Each of us is like a turtle on a fence post. We didn't
arrive at a place of success by ourselves. It's a result of God's
goodness and generosity, and we can only take credit for how
we've cooperated with God's plan by obeying Him.

Scripture says, "Both riches and honor come from
Thee, and Thou dost rule over all, and in Thy hand is power
and might; and it lies in Thy hand to make great, and to
strengthen everyone" (1 Chronicles 29:12).

6. *The contented woman understands that success need not
bring guilt or resentment.* As Solomon wisely wrote, "There is
futility which is done on the earth, that is, there are righteous
men to whom it happens according to the deeds of the
wicked. On the other hand, there are evil men to whom it
happens according to the deeds of the righteous. I say that

this too is futility" (Ecclesiastes 8:14).

When I'm experiencing a lack of major trials, I can easily feel guilty when other Christians around me are being bombarded by them. I might also feel resentful when I observe unbelievers prospering and seemingly not being punished for their evil.

Contentment can overcome those negative reactions as I remember I'm not responsible for what is happening to other people. God has every right to work in a completely different way in the life of each person. I need not feel guilty or resentful. I need only concentrate on God's faithfulness and then obey Him in the circumstances He's placed me in. The final act of world history has not been written, but in the end God's justice will be evident to all.

Solomon writes in Ecclesiastes 8:11-12, "Because the sentence against an evil deed is not executed quickly, therefore the hearts of the sons of men among them are given fully to do evil. Although a sinner does evil a hundred times and may lengthen his life, still I know that it will be well for those who fear God, who fear Him openly."

7. *The contented woman understands that success is to be enjoyed.* "Go then, eat your bread in happiness, and drink your wine with a cheerful heart; for God has already approved your works. . . . Whatever your hand finds to do, verily, do it with all your might" (Ecclesiastes 9:7,10).

God delights in blessing us with this time of success! His hand of goodness is upon us now, has been upon us in the past in the midst of trials, and will be upon us in the future, even if adversity returns. We can freely enjoy what He's given us, for He "has already approved your works." He has made it possible for us to enjoy what we're doing and if He didn't want us to do it, we wouldn't be able to enjoy it. In the vernacular of today, He's saying, "Contented woman: go for it!" And as someone else has said, "Live life to the hilt!"

God's Goodness

And why are we experiencing these blessings? Because of God's goodness. When we're tempted to take credit for our good fortune, we must remember that "every good thing bestowed and every perfect gift is from above, coming down from the Father of lights, with whom there is no variation, or shifting shadow" (James 1:17).

God's goodness was evident the very first day of creation when He created light and "saw that the light was good" (Genesis 1:4). On that day and since then, everything He's created is good. It is not possible for God to create anything that's not good, for His very being is "good." In Exodus 33:19, God tells Moses, "I Myself will make all My goodness pass before you." Then in Exodus 34:6, God passes before Moses and proclaims, "The LORD, the LORD God, compassionate and gracious, slow to anger, and abounding in lovingkindness and truth." The word *lovingkindness* in the original Hebrew refers to goodness.

Unger's Bible Dictionary defines goodness as "the supreme benevolence, holiness, and excellence of the divine character, the sum of all God's attributes."[4]

Dwelling on God's goodness will keep us content as we remember that success is a "good gift" from God that we haven't earned or deserved.

It's now been several years since any major trial has struck my life. Oh, yes, there have been stressful and painful incidents. My life hasn't been perfect. God has used even those circumstances to draw me closer to Him. But I no longer feel as if there's an ax of doom suspended over my head, just waiting for God's go-ahead to fall and clobber me. That doesn't mean something unfortunate won't happen. It just means I no longer live in fear that it will. I stand on the words of Solomon: "Have no fear of sudden disaster or of the ruin that overtakes the wicked, for the LORD will be your confidence and will keep your foot from being snared" (Proverbs 3:25-26, NIV).

I thank God for these years of respite from traumas and I acknowledge that they are His gift, not something I deserve. My contentment stems from a trust in His goodness. This has been a wonderful time, but if BIG trials should come, I know He'll supply whatever I need for them.

If you're experiencing a time of "success," I hope you'll find the same assurance.

NOTES: 1. Dr. James C. Dobson, "Dr. Dobson's Prescription for a Successful Marriage," *Focus on the Family Magazine* (October 1987), page 3, taken from Dr. James C. Dobson, *Love for a Lifetime* (Portland, Oreg.: Multnomah Press, 1987), used by permission.
2. Frank Minirth, Don Hawkins, Paul Meier, and Richard Flournoy, *How to Beat Burnout* (Chicago: Moody Press, 1986), page 77.
3. Allan C. Emery, *A Turtle On a Fencepost* (Waco, Tex.: Word, Inc., 1979), pages 13-14.
4. Merrill F. Unger, *Unger's Bible Dictionary* (Chicago: Moody Press, 1957, 1985), page 420.

10
Contentment During Mid-Life

I attended the meeting of an organization Larry and I belonged to even though Larry's work schedule prevented him from going for several months. Several new people were there, and one attractive man named Paul asked whether the seat beside me was taken. I replied, "No, please help yourself. My husband couldn't make it this time."

"Oh, my wife couldn't come either," he hastily added.

After the meeting when Paul talked to me, I felt important because he gave me his complete attention. At the next meeting, Paul immediately came over to me when I arrived and we had fun talking. Over the ensuing weeks, I thought of Paul during the week and looked forward to the meetings.

At one point when I was daydreaming about Paul, the thought slunk into my mind, "I wonder what it would be like to be married to him." All of a sudden, warning bells resounded through my being: "Kathy, what in the world are you thinking? You know you're perfectly happy married to Larry. He's the most wonderful thing in your life. Don't you dare give someone else a thought!"

I felt ashamed. What was missing in my life that the desire for someone else could take hold of me? I determined then and there to reject warm thoughts of Paul. But it wasn't easy, and seeing him weekly didn't help. I knew I needed to do something drastic.

The next week, I avoided Paul completely. When I saw him come toward me, I walked the other way and talked with someone else. For several weeks, I stayed away from him. I didn't want to hurt his feelings, but I didn't know of any other way to handle the situation.

I thought I should tell him why I was avoiding him, but I didn't have the courage. I'm glad I didn't. Several months later, a friend of mine told me she met a man from her Sunday school class for lunch to probe the reasons why she felt attracted to him. That "fact-finding" luncheon resulted in a sexual affair.

As time passed, I found myself thinking less and less about Paul. Now I can talk with Paul in a friendly way and not feel any attraction.

A year after this occurred, I shared a bit of this former struggle at a Bible study. One of the women told me, "I couldn't believe it when you shared that. I thought I was the only one. I think any man who pays attention to me is madly in love with me."

That woman is in her mid-thirties and I'm in my late thirties, yet what we were both experiencing could be a part of mid-life temptations. Although a crisis is often a part of "mid-life," we can choose whether it will become a normal transition or a time of crisis.

In this chapter we'll be looking at several aspects of mid-life: adjusting to an "empty nest," caring for an elderly parent, coping with a husband's mid-life crisis, or dealing with your own.

Empty Nest

Becky didn't know if she'd be content after her two children went off to college. Her friends were convinced she wouldn't be. "I put so much time into my kids that my friends told me, 'You won't be able to handle your children leaving.' But people are surprised how well I've adjusted. I really believe contentment and letting go are related. I've been letting go even while being very involved.

"When each of my kids started first grade, they were responsible for getting themselves out of bed with their alarm clock. When my daughter started driving, I insisted she make her own dentist, hair, and doctor appointments. I think I'm content now because I've taught my kids to be resourceful. Discontent stems from worrying that they aren't prepared for the world. When my children were thirteen and fifteen, I told them, 'I don't know how parents can let their children go.' The Lord has obviously strengthened me.

"When they became adults, I became their adviser. I've done everything I could; now the world has to teach them the rest. If they fall, that's fine; their dad and I are here to help, but we aren't in the same role we were in when they were growing up.

"It boils down to: Am I going to worry about them or am I going to trust God to work in their lives? Knowing that He's in control and that He loves them helps me release them to His care.

"With the kids gone, I need to concentrate on my husband's needs. The temptation for me is to serve others instead of my husband. I'm very service-oriented and my husband isn't. If there's any struggle I have right now, it's finding a balance between meeting my husband's needs and still fulfilling my desire to reach out to others."

Christian psychologist Clyde Narramore addresses the empty nest syndrome: "When the children were small, you were more than occupied with responsibilities pertaining to them; now that they are grown and are on their own, it has left an empty void.

"Your restlessness and feelings of frustration are very understandable. While you were raising your children, you knew that you were needed and you knew what your purpose and goals were. It is time now to reevaluate your life and set new goals."[1]

You may want to consider going back to college to finish a degree or begin a new one. Or maybe a full-time or part-time job would challenge you. There's also the possibility of community work or volunteering to help some Christian organization or missions group. Try taking some tests through your local counseling service to determine your temperament or personality type and what areas might be of interest to you.

Look at this time as positive and as an opportunity for you to strengthen your relationships with your husband and friends, and to increase your ministry potential. And remember, God can accomplish more through a woman who may be unsure of her talents but who is available to Him than through a multi-talented Christian who is resistant to His purposes.

Empty Nest No Longer Empty

Tina's children had been away from home for several years when her daughter, Shelly, asked to return home to complete graduate studies at a nearby Christian college. Tina and her husband welcomed her back, but not without a few pangs of regret. "I had enjoyed the empty nest. The house stayed the way I wanted it. Yet I also found out my husband and I created messes we couldn't blame on the children.

"When my daughter returned, I expected her to clean up after herself but she didn't. She expected me to continue to mother her. As a friend of mine says, 'When the children come back, they want you to mother them on their terms. They don't want to be told what to do but they want to be cared for. They want the privileges without the responsibilities.' With Shelly, I finally had to say, 'This isn't fair.' Then we each discussed our expectations.

"We've had to make some adjustments. She got her own phone because I was constantly taking her messages. I also had to learn to release her when she stayed out late at night. At first, I'd stay awake worrying. Then I realized I needed my sleep, so I gave her to the Lord and now I don't even hear her when she comes in.

"But there are some definite advantages to having her here. I've enjoyed relating to her as an adult.

"When I start to get discontented, I remind myself that it's just for a short time and that it was our decision to allow her to return. That keeps resentment away."

Tina is fortunate that her relationship with her children is a positive one. It doesn't always work out that way. Jean is experiencing the return of her daughter, Kim, her son-in-law, and grandbaby into her home and there isn't much contentment. Kim agreed to help with housework but thinks five minutes of effort is enough. Plus, they haven't contributed any money and Jean's husband is out of work. Even though they've discussed what everyone is supposed to do, the "children" haven't cooperated and Jean's husband gave them thirty days to leave. Jean has fought the feeling of guilt for kicking them out with the baby, but she says, "It's the only way they're going to learn."

Jean has had to learn contentment by resisting false guilt. She realizes she is not responsible for providing for the needs of her daughter and family. "Tough love" is often the first step toward contentment.

Caring for an Elderly Parent

Lorrie's mother, LuAnn, died when she was eighty-seven, after spending four years in Lorrie's home. "For the first two years Mother lived in our home, I was not content with our decision to have her here. I became angry at my husband, Roger, because he felt it was God's will for her to come. But when it didn't turn out well, I blamed Roger and God for my discontent.

"Mother had physical problems, but her mind was very clear. She'd tell me where to put the furniture. I'd get angry because I felt like a teenager again. Then I'd ask her forgiveness for my anger, but she wouldn't talk to me. Even though Mother had become a Christian at age eighty-one, she wasn't able to let Christ change a lot of her attitudes.

"My first breakthrough toward contentment came when I took Betty Coble's class called 'Woman Aware and Choosing.' Betty said that I was to honor my mother but that I no longer had to obey her. Therefore, when Mother said something that before would have made me feel like a child, I could think, 'Well, that's your opinion, and I don't have to do it unless I think it's correct.'

"Another area I gained contentment in was not feeling guilty about leaving Mother. Now I could put my husband before her. I no longer had to make her a part of every area of my life. And when she would pout, I realized she would have to choose her own happiness. I released myself from trying to meet all her needs. As my attitudes changed, I was less irritable and more ready to hug and kiss her and say 'I love you.'

"My definition of contentment is submitting to God's will for me at any point in life. It's trusting Him to provide for my needs regardless of what He brings. The opposite of contentment is fighting His will and wanting a different situation. I'm so glad I allowed the Lord to bring contentment into my life so that those last years with my mother were good ones."

Ruby is another woman who chose contentment while caring for an elderly mother—for fifteen years. She comments, "How was I content while caring for my mother? Well, I wasn't always. Many times I wanted to do my own thing and not deliver Mother and several little old ladies to their meetings. When I grew weary physically, the enemy quickly spread the table for a pity party. I got tired of fixing extra meals, doing extra wash, running to the doctors. Whenever my focus became ingrown I became discontented.

"But God in His grace was at work in me and used those priceless years as an investment—not just for my precious mother, but also as a personal one for me. The truths He taught me as I sought Him and His Word enlightened and strengthened me. Remaining in the Scriptures was my life-saver, for there He trained me so that I could be adequate and fully equipped to serve Him in this way.

"One time when I felt discouraged, the faithful Holy Spirit recharged my spiritual batteries with 1 Timothy 5:4: 'If any widow has children or grandchildren, let them first learn to practice piety in regard to their own family, and to make some return to their parents; for this is acceptable in the sight of God.'

"'Lord,' I cried out, 'I'm doing what pleases You. What more could I want?' And when Mother falteringly said, 'I'm such a bother,' I lovingly, laughingly replied, 'Oh, Mother,

no way! I'm "requiting," as the *King James Version* says.'
That put it all in a new perspective, and contentment began
simmering in my soul."

A Husband in Mid-Life Crisis

Sherrie couldn't believe it when her Christian husband said
he wanted a divorce. Of all people, she never figured it would
happen to her. Sherrie says, "James Dobson talks about a
rejected person feeling like an old shoe someone throws out. I
felt like that old shoe. The person who was supposed to love
me most said he no longer did, and my self-esteem hit
bottom.

"I kept asking, 'Why?' I never got any answer from God
or Jim. All Jim could say was, 'I've been doing for you and
Jeff all my life. Now I'm going to do for myself.' Now I
realize he was in a mid-life crisis. He couldn't change his
work situation so he changed his family in an effort to wipe
out his vague dissatisfaction with life.

"But at the time, that didn't answer my why question. I
wanted to know how God could allow such a devastation in
my life. Then my pastor preached, 'God asks us, "If I never
show you the reason why, will you trust Me?"' I knew God
was asking me, 'If you never know why, will you trust Me
enough or fret throughout your life?' I chose to learn contentment and to release my need to know why.

"Contentment to me is being at peace in your circumstances even if they aren't what you've chosen. It's the opposite of grumbling constantly. I'm content because I know I
was willing to do anything to make our marriage work, but
Jim wasn't willing. I couldn't make him. All I can do is be
willing to let God work in me.

"Although I've chosen to have contentment, I still
struggle with some things. My main struggle is fighting
bitterness over the relationship between my son and his dad.

Jeff is a senior in high school and his dad isn't there for him emotionally. My son views it as rejection and it tears my heart apart to see him hurting.

"Isaiah 54:11,13 has become a real solace to me: 'O afflicted one, storm-tossed, and not comforted . . . all your sons will be taught of the LORD; and the well-being of your sons will be great.'"

Sherrie's husband chose divorce as the way to handle his mid-life crisis, but not all husbands do. Janice's husband, Jack, stayed in the marriage and is making everyone miserable. Especially Janice. She laments, "Jack is so depressed . . . and depressing. He doesn't have much love for me or the girls. He says he's discouraged about his job and I try to listen, but when I share my needs he doesn't want to hear it. It seems like I'm trying to hold the family together all by myself.

"It helps me if I focus on the positives. Plus I know the Lord has drawn me closer to Him through this. But I'm very concerned about the girls. They aren't getting the emotional nourishment they need. They ask him, 'Why aren't you smiling, Daddy?'

"It's taking all my effort to choose contentment and trust God. I hope God strengthens me to hang on until Jack works through his problems."

People like Janice need help, and mid-life experts Jim and Sally Conway give these suggestions for wives whose husbands are experiencing a mid-life crisis:

1. Understand the problem.
2. Be prepared for widely vacillating moods.
3. Be prepared to be blamed for your husband's depression.
4. Be attractive.
5. Find ways to gently draw your husband out of his cave of silence.

6. Build his self-image.
7. Encourage him to attempt new areas of growth.
8. Keep yourself emotionally strong.[2]

After studying more about mid-life crisis, Janice was more content in allowing Jack to move through his transitions. She no longer felt a need to "fix" his problems. She realized that trying to force him into a quick solution would only put unneeded stress on him. For almost a year she looked to God to strengthen her and it paid off. Little by little, Jack became interested in life and her again. Although, they're not out of the woods completely.

"I don't know what I would have done if I hadn't learned to not take Jack's problem personally. By refusing to blame myself or become defensive, I could actually be more supportive of him. When he would try to blame me, I'd say something like, 'I'm sure it does seem like my fault to you, but I won't take all the blame. I'm willing to work with you on whatever is needed to heal our relationship.' I'm so glad there were books and people available to help me stay strong."

Women's Mid-Life Woes

"I felt so frustrated," writes Sally Conway, "and my husband just lay there, going off to sleep. I wanted him to talk to me, but I didn't know how to bring it about without making him angry.

"Besides, when we did talk, I couldn't seem to help him understand me. I just got more confused and frustrated, and we usually ended up with bad feelings toward each other. I had a busy day tomorrow, but my daily life seemed part of another world.

"That gnawing uneasiness I had felt off and on all day [grew] stronger and stronger. I wanted to share it with Jim and have him help me get rid of it. . . . I felt left out and unneeded, like a discarded old box.

"A wave of self-pity would wash over me. Right after that, a bigger wave of jealousy would slam into me. And before I could get myself righted from that blow, a third wave of just plain rejection and hurt would hit me. An old box—yes, I felt like a soggy cardboard box.

"But I didn't want to sink! Well, yes, often I did want to vanish from life, but what I really wanted was for all the inner confusion I felt to be straightened out so I could get on with the happy life I was supposed to be living. Part of me was happy, but a big chunk of me was miserable, and I didn't know why.

"Experiences like this were common to me, off and on, during the last half of my thirties. My frustration and confusion were especially critical from about age thirty-six through thirty-nine. I thought the problem was simply unique to me—some personal quirks I needed to work out. Now [I] see that the problem was my transition into mid-life."[3]

Sally's words describe thousands of women who are experiencing discontent as they face mid-life. Discontent often is the main characteristic of those years, and yet it doesn't have to be that way. Achieving contentment can prevent a transition from becoming a crisis.

In their newest book, *Your Marriage Can Survive Mid-Life Crisis*, the Conways explain the difference between a transition and a crisis by saying, "A transition means that a person moves from one era or stage of life to another. Transitions take place several times during life, such as when moving from being a child to an adolescent or from being a mid-life adult to a mellow adult. Each of these movements, if properly understood and planned for, can take place without an overwhelming amount of stress.

"However, if several stress factors converge at the same

time the transition is taking place, a crisis can be produced.

"Every man and woman will go through the transition from being a young adult to being a mid-life adult. Not all of them will have a crisis. Our studies show, however, that more than two-thirds of the women and around 75 to 80 percent of the men in America do. This means that for a period of time they do not function as usual. They eventually make an extensive evaluation of their life's direction that causes shifts in their values and pursuits."[4]

There are many stress factors that can cause a woman's mid-life crisis. Some of them are:

1. Our present-day cultural view of women.
2. An unhappy marital situation or lack of a marriage.
3. Her husband's own mid-life crisis.
4. Demands from children and their growing independence.
5. Career priorities related to other life priorities.
6. An accumulation of traumatic losses such as death, illness, or aging.
7. Urgency from her inner clocks to accomplish her life dreams.
8. Imperative reevaluation time to review the past and plan the future.[5]

During these years, a woman's thoughts may be: "Who am I?" "Where do I go from here?" "My body has let me down." "Why am I doing what I'm doing?" "I'm all alone."

Sally says, "Discontent does bubble up at mid-life, even in those who were content before. Formerly, a woman may have kept hoping her expectations would materialize, but she now sees some were unrealistic and will never come true. Now too many stresses converge on her and cause emotional weariness. Her former coping mechanisms no longer work and she begins to dwell upon her dissatisfactions.

"For instance, maybe her marriage is a sore spot and she keeps thinking it'll get better. But by mid-life, it hasn't gotten better and she loses hope. Discontent overwhelms her.

"I believe we keep contentment going by inches. For me personally, I've noticed that I must seek the Lord moment by moment, whereas I used to be able to just have my quiet time and go on about my day. Now I must constantly seek Him so that I don't give in to discontent.

"We must realize, though, that discontent can have its positive side during this time. Discontent may make a woman evaluate her lifestyle and realize she needs to make some changes. Not all that happens in a crisis is bad. It can create positive changes. Contentment says I'm at rest with my circumstances but I don't have to be satisfied with the way they are. It's okay for me to make changes as the Lord leads.

"First Timothy 6:6 tells us, 'But godliness actually is a means of great gain, when accompanied by contentment.' I think that means being God-conscious about what we're doing and accepting things that might otherwise have caused discontentment in us. Contentment is a result of constantly looking at life from God's perspective, believing God is right here with me."[6]

King David

The term "mid-life" isn't mentioned in the Bible, but there is a biblical character we may be able to identify as going through a mid-life crisis. It's King David. In 2 Samuel 11:1-2,4-5, we read, "Then it happened in the spring, at the time when kings go out to battle, that David . . . stayed at Jerusalem. Now when evening came David arose from his bed and walked around on the roof of the king's house, and from the roof he saw a woman bathing; and the woman was very beautiful in appearance. . . . David sent messengers and took her, and when she came to him, he lay with her; and when she had purified herself from her uncleanness, she returned to her house. And the woman conceived; and she sent and told David, and said, 'I am pregnant.'"

The story continues as David has Bathsheba's husband, Uriah, killed in battle to cover up his sin. Bathsheba becomes David's wife and gives birth to a son who dies as God's judgment.

Although we don't know for sure that David's situation was caused by a mid-life crisis, it does have several elements often involved in mid-life: irresponsibility, discontent, temptation, adultery, and consequences.

But just as there was a happy ending to David's story with the birth of Solomon, so there can be a smooth transition through mid-life for each of us. The ingredient we need is God's strength.

God's Strength

When we begin to ask some of those mid-life questions, our strength ebbs and the old coping tools grow weak. We need God's strength in an even greater way to deal with the increasing stresses on our lives. Philippians 4:13 offers hope: "I can do all things through Him who strengthens me."

God's strength is available so that we can:

Evaluate. We need to ask ourselves these questions: Do I have needs that aren't being met? How can they be met? Which needs can people meet and which needs can only God meet? Do I have unhealed emotional wounds, hurtful relationships, glossed-over dissatisfactions, unfulfilled dreams, or losses I haven't worked through? What can I begin doing to solve these problems? What plans should I make to improve my future and my outlook on it: college, additional training, physical fitness, ministry opportunities?

Take action. We need to put into action the plans we've made and verbalize our needs to those around us with "I messages" rather than blaming other people. We should delegate overwhelming responsibilities, give more independence to our children, and hold them accountable with effective discipline. We can remind our husbands of our needs but ultimately look to God as the complete answer.

Be realistic. We must give up unrealistic expectations that everything will become perfect or that all areas of dissatisfaction will vanish. We must understand it will take time for our plans to become effective and take small steps in several areas instead of a big step in one area. We must commit ourselves to choosing contentment over a period of time.

Seek God. We need to make our spiritual life a high priority, committing ourselves to daily interaction with God and ministry to others. We must decide to obey even though an ungodly choice may seem a more immediate solution to our needs. We should be open to counsel from other godly Christians.

These four steps can work toward a smooth transition into mid-life and can also help in pulling someone out of a crisis. They can also help us choose contentment during this most important time of life.

NOTES: 1. Clyde Narramore, "Answers to Your Questions," *Psychology for Living* (May 1984), page 12.
2. Jim and Sally Conway, *Maximize Your Mid-Life* (Wheaton, Ill.: Tyndale House Publishers, 1987), pages 31-33, used by permission.
3. Conway, *Maximize Your Mid-Life,* pages 5-7, used by permission.
4. Jim and Sally Conway, *Your Marriage Can Survive Mid-Life Crisis* (Wheaton, Ill.: Tyndale House Publishers, 1987), pages 12-13.

5. Jim and Sally Conway, *Women in Mid-Life Crisis* (Wheaton, Ill.: Tyndale House Publishers, 1983), page 20, used by permission.
6. From a personal interview I had with Sally Conway.

11
The Fruit of Contentment

We're almost finished in our journey toward contentment. I don't know about you, but after I've read a book or attended a seminar or heard a sermon, I sometimes wonder, "What did I actually learn, anyway?" Maybe there was so much information that it's hard to process it all.

If you feel that way about this book, it might help to review. Then we'll discover what characteristics you can expect to see in your life as a result of choosing contentment.

In Review
In the first chapter, I described the discontented person and invited you to join me on this adventure toward the content-

ment God wants for all of us.

In the second, we discovered some of the myths about contentment: that it's based on perfection, it's the same as positive thinking and happiness, and it comes upon us while we passively wait.

The third chapter helped us see that contentment starts with knowing Jesus Christ as Lord and Savior and that there's a difference between contentment and satisfaction.

For the remaining chapters, let's look at this chart:

Chapter	Topic	God's Character	Example	Scripture
4.	Physical Characteristics	Wisdom	Moses	Psalm 139
5.	Stress	Faithfulness	Israelites	Habakkuk 3:17-18
6.	Trials	Sovereignty	Joseph	Romans 8:16-39
7.	Relationships	Love	Paul and Barnabas	Ephesians 3:17-19
8.	Physical Affliction	Mercy	Paul	2 Corinthians 12:7-10
9.	Success	Goodness	Solomon	Ecclesiastes
10.	Mid-Life	Strength	David	Philippians 4:13

I hope reviewing this information will help you solidify the basic principles in your mind so that you can clearly know how to choose contentment.

The Enemies of Contentment

For much of our journey, we've looked at specific circumstances where we needed to gain contentment. Now we'll look at some temptations that can rob us of a contented spirit. If these enemies overwhelm us, this can be the result: "You have sown much, but harvest little; you eat, but there is not enough to be satisfied; you drink, but there is not enough to become drunk; you put on clothing, but no one is warm enough; and he who earns, earns wages to put into a purse with holes" (Haggai 1:6). That's quite an accurate description of discontent. We don't want that to happen to us, so let's examine the enemies: anxiety, grumbling, greed, and jealousy.

Anxiety. When we're anxious, we're not content. We aren't focusing on God's wisdom, faithfulness, sovereignty, love, mercy, goodness, and strength.

Instead, we need to think of Paul's exhortation in Philippians 4:6-7: "Be anxious for nothing, but in everything by prayer and supplication with thanksgiving let your requests be made known to God. And the peace of God, which surpasses all comprehension, shall guard your hearts and your minds in Christ Jesus."

Paul gives us a plan for dealing with anxiety. Here's how I use it. Just the other day, Larry and I were preparing for him to meet with the IRS for our first income tax audit in seventeen years of marriage. As we tried to find all the receipts of our deductions and remember what in the world we spent $22.18 on three years ago, I started getting anxious. I feared that we'd have to pay thousands of dollars. (Isn't that just like anxiety? It makes us build every molehill into a mountain.)

After I realized I was feeling nervous, I prayed, "Lord, this is getting to me. I know we haven't done anything wrong, but how are we going to prove it? Right now I turn all of this over to You and pray for Your favor upon Larry as he meets with that auditor. I've been reading about Joseph in Genesis and how You gave him favor and I'm asking for the same thing. Please be in charge of this and help Larry as he prepares. Thank You for helping us."

Each time I started to get nervous, I prayed a similar prayer and turned it back over to the Lord. In the past when I've been so anxious about something that even prayer doesn't release me, I'll fight a spiritual battle and say out loud, "Almighty God, in Jesus' name and power, I bind

Satan from attacking me any longer." It amazes me each time
how such assertiveness will usually wipe away the feeling of
anxiety and fear that has gripped my heart. As a result, God's
peace supernaturally assures me that He will take care of the
situation.

And that's exactly what happened with the IRS audit.
Larry went into the office prepared and the auditor started
out very gruff and uncooperative. Larry showed him some
minor corrections, some of which were to our disadvantage
and some to our advantage. By the time the two hours were
over, the auditor was cordial and helpful, even showing
Larry how to write up a deduction so he could get a better
benefit the next time.

The end result: we didn't have to pay anything. Larry
said it must have been my prayers. Those prayers also helped
me eliminate anxiety and thus stay content.

Grumbling. Grumbling describes a discontented person.
It's the woman who complains and doesn't notice all the
blessings in her life. Philippians 2:14 says, "Do all things
without grumbling or disputing." Grumbling doesn't get us
anywhere.

Instead, we should correct the situation that's creating
our discontent. If it can't be corrected, we need to surrender
our desires to the Lord and choose to be content in the midst
of it.

I recently needed to eliminate grumbling from my life
when I became discontented about Larry's lack of enthusi-
asm to purchase a replacement part for my computer. The
word processing worked fine without it but required a little
more effort on my part. I reminded him several times and felt
defensive and angry. Why wasn't he sensitive to my needs?
Then I told him that if he didn't buy it by a certain date, I
would buy it myself. The date came and went, and as I
worked on the computer and became efficient at a few more

key strokes, the importance of that part lessened. I knew I could go buy the part and be justified in doing so since we had the money, but somehow I never got around to it. It didn't seem as important as before. A sense of contentment replaced my grumbling.

Almost nine months later, Larry learned that the replacement part had been improved, so he bought it shortly after. As I enjoyed my new abilities to use my computer, I thanked God for the contentment He had given me. For if I had demanded replacing the part when I'd originally wanted it, I would not be enjoying the extra capabilities of the improved part.

I also learned from that experience that what seems so very important and is the reason for my grumbling, can often lessen in importance as time passes. Therefore, it may not be a bad idea to let a little time go by to see whether something is really important enough to "go to battle over." Now that doesn't mean I shouldn't be assertive in expressing my needs. But grumbling along with that expression most likely won't help to get my point across.

Greed. Wanting more than we have, with an attitude of "I must have this in order to be content," is greed. Greed is not just desiring things; it's wanting them no matter what God wants. Greed can encompass any area, not just the area of material possessions. Christians can become greedy about other Christians' spiritual gifts or God-given talents, their sense of humor, or their physical appearance.

To ward off greed, we need to have an attitude that says, "I'd like this, Lord, yet not my will, but Yours." Hebrews 13:5-6 warns us, "Let your character be free from the love of money, being content with what you have; for He Himself has said, 'I will never desert you, nor will I ever forsake you,' so that we confidently say, 'The Lord is my helper, I will not be afraid, what shall man do to me?'"

Notice the verse says, "Be free from the *love* of money." It doesn't say, "Be free from money." If we love money for its own sake, we can slide quickly into greed, but if we look to God to use money to meet our needs and minister to others, we have the right perspective. Greediness says, "God has deserted me; He has forsaken me. I must provide for myself." Contentment says, "God hasn't forsaken me, even if everything I think I need isn't provided. He loves me and will provide for my true needs."

Jealousy. James 3:16 says, "Where jealousy and selfish ambition exist, there is disorder and every evil thing." Jealousy can be defined as an attitude of resentful suspicion. Dwelling on suspicious ideas, being overprotective, or demanding unreasonable loyalty can push us into jealousy. Discontent will follow close behind.

Fighting jealous thoughts doesn't mean hiding from facts that may need to be dealt with—the unfaithfulness of a husband, for instance. But dwelling on suspicions without taking action to see whether the suspicions are true will never banish jealousy. The solution is to examine the jealous thought, discuss it with a godly friend or counselor, and determine its validity. If it's true, take action. If it's not true, reject the thought by reminding yourself of what is true and reaffirming your ultimate trust in the Lord. Then contentment can return.

These four enemies—anxiety, grumbling, greed, and jealousy—can turn contentment into discontent. Since we don't want these kinds of rotten fruit in our lives, we'll choose contentment with God's power and grow delicious godly fruit instead.

The Fruit of Contentment

Charles D. Kelley defines contentment as "the God-given ability to be satisfied with the loving provision of God in any and every situation."[1] Someone else has said that it's "an uncomplaining acceptance of one's share." The roots of the tree of contentment are grounded in faith that God is in control and acceptance of what He provides. Let's look now at the kind of "fruit" that will grow from the limbs of our contented spirits.

Love

When I'm content, I'm more loving because I don't have to change other people. I know it's God's responsibility to change them, not mine.

In our chapter on relationships, we learned about unconditional love and disapproval. We found out that we can still love someone even as we express our disapproval about something he or she has done.

I'm challenged to reject the thought that withholding love from someone will make that person change. Being content means I've accepted God's unconditional love and know He's still changing me. If He can do that in my life, He's powerful enough to do it in another person's life. I'll let Him.

Carole put these principles into practice after she had a disagreement with her husband, Tim, over the way to discipline their teenaged son. She didn't feel very loving toward Tim but chose to enjoy his lovemaking that evening. It was the first time she'd been able to make such a decision of love. She says, "As a result, God gave me a supernatural contentment, knowing we wouldn't straighten everything out about Jason in one evening. I realized my relationship with Tim was more important than any disagreement."

Joy

When I'm content, I'm more joyful because I'm trusting that God is in control.

Joy and contentment are closely related. They are both based on the confidence that God is sovereign even though my circumstances may not seem like a reason for rejoicing. Neither joy nor contentment are dependent upon positive circumstances. Even if the situations surrounding me are unpleasant, I can still make the decision to be content and joyful.

One Christmas season, ten-year-old Mark asked for a set of golf clubs after starting lessons. He constantly asked me what Larry would get him, fearful and unhappy that he might not receive what he wanted, which was a full set.

I replied, "Honey, Daddy will get you whatever you truly need. Daddy knows what's best for you and will get the number of clubs necessary for you to learn golf. That might not be a full set, Mark, but your dad will do the right thing."

After Mark mulled that over, he returned to his cheerful self.

Peace

When I'm content, I'm more peaceful because I know God wants the best for me.

The opposite of peace is anxiety, the fear that God can't truly be trusted to do the right thing for me. Anxiety tells my inner being:

- that I should manipulate and control my circumstances;
- that I need to make other people do what I think so that I'll feel secure;
- that I need to have everything perfect to show that I really am okay;
- that I need to keep on my mask so that other people can't see the real me, a person who has hurts and struggles like them.

Peace, on the other hand, allows God to be in control while I actively pursue what He wants me to do. It's the confidence that God does know what He's doing in my life.

Saint Francis de Sales said, "Do not look forward to the trials and crosses of this life with dread and fear. Rather, look to them with full confidence that, as they arise, God, to whom you belong, will deliver you from them.

"He has guided and guarded you thus far in life. Do you but hold fast to His dear hand, and He will lead you safely through all trials. Whenever you cannot stand, He will carry you lovingly in His arms.

"Do not look forward to what may happen tomorrow. The same Eternal Father who cares for you today will take good care of you tomorrow and every day of your life. Either He will shield you from suffering or He will give you the unfailing strength to bear it.

"Be at peace then and put aside all useless thoughts, vain dreads, and anxious imaginations."

Patience

When I'm content, I'm more patient because I know God has His own schedule.

As a result, I'm more patient with people even when they—or I—don't improve the way I think we should. I can pass along patience to them and myself because God has been patient with my growth process. Contentment and patience lead me to relax in God's schedule, even when interruptions seem to be preventing me from doing what I'd planned. Patience is truly believing that God's power will give me eventual victory in an area of sin and that He who has begun a good work in me will complete it (Philippians 1:6).

One of my favorite sayings is, "God will give me enough time to do what He wants me to do." My part is to obey Him as I go through my day. When interruptions come, I must ask

God for wisdom as I decide whether to reject the interference or allow it to change my plans. Most often I perceive that God has a different plan than I do. As a result, I can patiently respond to that interruption, whether it's a sick child or a friend asking for a ride to the doctor's office.

Contentment and patience won in a spiritual battle I fought when I took a taxi from where I was staying to a TV interview. The seventy-eight-year-old driver said we'd arrive at the station in thirty minutes, but he lost his way. As we drove around taking longer and longer to find the TV station, I felt angry and impatient. I wanted him to feel bad for the problems he was causing me.

When we were still lost at the time I was supposed to be at the program, the words of a song began swimming through my brain: "Save each man's dignity and save each man's pride." I knew I didn't have the words completely right but the message was definitely getting through. This elderly gentleman's dignity was more important than getting to that program on time.

I turned my attention to the Lord and asked Him to forgive me for my lack of trust in Him. I reminded myself that God evidently had a different time schedule. As a result, I could talk calmly with the driver and even told him about God's love for him. If I'd been impatient, I would have misrepresented God.

We finally arrived at the studio an hour late and taped the interview program anyway. I thanked God for the patience He'd given me and that the program hadn't been live.

Kindness, Goodness, and Gentleness

When I'm content, I'm more kind, good, and gentle because I can concentrate on the needs of others. Since I know God will meet my needs, I don't have to focus on me and can be absorbed with reaching out to others with caring words and actions. My goal is to see God glorified as I represent His goodness. My thinking changes from "How can I get what I think I need?" to "How would Jesus react in this situation?"

Several weeks ago as I drove to my weekly bowling league, I prayed, "Lord, help me to represent You by being loving and kind." As the morning went along, I tried to be encouraging to the opposing team by praising them when they bowled well. At one point, one of their team members said to me, "You're a very encouraging person." Even though I didn't have the opportunity to share the Lord with her at that moment, I thanked God that He had answered my prayer.

Although I'm not able to forget about my needs all the time, I notice that the more content I am, the easier it is to be sensitive to the needs of others. And when I express my needs to others, I'm more willing to see their side of the story.

Faithfulness and Self-Control

When I'm content, I'm more faithful and self-controlled because I'm empowered by God.

Faithfulness is dependability in doing good; self-control is doing that good in God's power. Because I'm believing God has control over my life (that's contentment), I also believe He has the power that helps me in situations that seem beyond my abilities. My confidence is not in myself but in the Holy Spirit who indwells me.

For example, the other day I volunteered to take a meal to the family of an acquaintance, Joyce, after a mutual friend found out that Joyce was in the hospital. At the time it seemed to fit into my schedule, but as my assigned day approached, I could think of all sorts of reasons to try to get out of it. My desire to be faithful waned, even though I really wanted to please the Lord. In effect, "The spirit was willing, but the flesh was weak."

As I prepared the food, my attitude wasn't very loving and I kept praying something like, "Well, Lord, You know my heart isn't in this but I believe doing it will please You and represent You to that family. So I acknowledge my weak desire and ask for Your power to be faithful and cheerful! I don't feel like it, but I'm willing to be made willing."

There wasn't any way I could *make* myself cheerful except to obey what I believed God wanted me to do. Larry wasn't home at that point or I could have expressed my feelings to him and that might have helped. Sharing with someone else often helps me work through my unpleasant feelings.

As I drove to Joyce's house, I kept setting my mind on God's interests instead of mine (Matthew 16:23), even though I still wasn't "feeling" like I wanted to be faithful. By the time I reached my destination, though, God did through His Spirit what I couldn't do. A cheerfulness about serving developed within me. Not only was I faithful in doing good, but I was able to control myself, thus being obedient with God's help.

Knowing that God wants the best for me, I'm content to let Him have His way. That means I release control of the way I want to react and allow Him to control my reactions. I do this by thinking, "I really want to blast Susie with my anger for gossiping about me, but since my deepest desire is to obey God, I'll confront her with her sin in a loving way."

Humility

When I'm content, I'm more humble because God is the source of anything I do that is worthy of praise.

As I accept the person God has made me to be—both my physical appearance and inner personality—I don't crave to see myself either promoted or put down. I can have an accurate assessment of myself even as God is changing me into the image of His Son Jesus Christ.

Galatians 6:3-4 tells us, "For if anyone thinks he is something when he is nothing, he deceives himself. But let each one examine his own work, and then he will have reason for boasting in regard to himself alone, and not in regard to another." Verse 4 in the *New International Version* reads, "Then he can take pride in himself, without comparing himself to somebody else."

Humility is not putting myself down; it is acknowledging the gifts and talents God put within me. Humility is not considering myself a worm, but viewing myself as a valuable creation of God. And yes, there is even reason for boasting about myself, but with the attitude that Paul had when he said, "Therefore in Christ Jesus I have found reason for boasting in things pertaining to God. For I will not presume to speak of anything except what Christ has accomplished through me" (Romans 15:17-18).

God's kind of humility within me can say "thank you" when someone gives me a compliment. God's kind of humility within me can rejoice in a hairstyle that prettily frames my face. God's kind of humility within me seeks the spiritual gifts that are waiting to be used for His glory.

The emphasis of this kind of humility is not "Look at *me!*" but "Isn't God wonderful? Look at the tremendous things He's done through me."

And even though our motive is not to be praised by men, God says that will often happen. Peter said, "Humble yourselves, therefore, under the mighty hand of God, that He may exalt you at the proper time" (1 Peter 5:6).

Several months ago, I attended a women's council meeting at my church, where various leaders met to report on their groups. I decided I would practice self-control and not say anything since I often share too quickly in a group and take away time from others. After several had shared, the chairman suddenly looked at me and said, "Oh, Kathy, you haven't shared yet." I felt at peace as I told of my current class. A few more ladies talked and then one woman said, "I just want to praise God for Kathy Miller's ministry." She continued to relate how much I had blessed her life. I was amazed. I barely knew her and couldn't really remember when I'd had much contact with her. I left the meeting, awed at God's timing. At a time when I determined to be humble, He lifted me up.

Faith

When I'm content, I have greater faith in God's abilities. When my faith in God is strong, I trust that what He's doing in me is for my good. Andrew Murray wrote, "You know how the eagle's wings are obtained. Only in one way—by the eagle's birth. You are born of God. You have the eagle's wings. You may not have known it; you may not have used them; but God can and will teach you to use them.

"You know how the eagles are taught the use of their wings. See yonder cliff rising a thousand feet out of the sea. See high up a ledge on the rock, where there is an eagle's nest with its treasure of two young eaglets. See the mother bird come and stir up her nest, and with her beak push the timid birds over the precipice. See how they flutter and fall and sink toward the depth. See now how she 'fluttereth over her young, spreadeth abroad her wings, taketh them, beareth them on her wings' (Deuteronomy 32:11), and so, as they ride upon her wings, brings them to a place of safety. And so she does once and again, each time casting them out over the precipice, and then again taking and carrying them.

"Yes, the instinct of that eagle mother was God's gift, a single ray of that love in which the Almighty trains His people to mount as on eagles' wings. He stirs up your nest. He disappoints your hopes. He brings down your confidence. He makes you fear and tremble, as all your strength fails, and you feel utterly weary and helpless. And all the while He is spreading His strong wings for you to rest your weakness on.

"All He asks is that you should sink down in your weariness and wait on Him; and allow Him to carry you as you ride upon the wings of His omnipotence."

When life is falling apart around me, contentment and faith assure me that God isn't falling apart. When I become discontented, in effect I think of God pacing the floor of Heaven, muttering, "Oh, no, what in the world is going on down there? I just don't know what I'm going to do about it. This has really got Me worried."

No, sister in Christ, God isn't worried! Daniel 2:20-22 assures us, "Let the name of God be blessed forever and ever, for wisdom and power belong to Him. And it is He who changes the times and the epochs; He removes kings and establishes kings; He gives wisdom to wise men, and knowledge to men of understanding. It is He who reveals the profound and hidden things; He knows what is in the darkness, and the light dwells with Him."

When your contentment and faith in God's abilities weaken, think of His characteristics in this manner: in ABC order. He is:

A—almighty;
B—beautiful;
C—compassionate, creative, caring;
D—determined, diligent;
E—efficient, everlasting, eager to save, eternal;
F—faithful, forgiving;
G—generous, great, gentle, giving, glorious, good;

H—honest, healing, holy;
I—interested in me, immortal, impartial;
J—joyful, jealous, just;
K—kind, kingly;
L—loving, loyal;
M—mighty, merciful, majestic;
N—never-ending;
O—omnipresent, omniscient;
P—powerful, persuasive, peaceful, patient;
Q—quiet;
R—righteous;
S—sovereign, slow to anger, strong, stable;
T—truthful, trustworthy;
U—universal, united;
V—victorious, virtuous;
W—wealthy, worthy to be praised, wise;
X—(e)xcellent;
Y—youthful;
Z—zealous.

You'll most likely be able to think of even more characteristics. Meditating on such a great God and adding more to this list is bound to increase your faith and restore your contentment.

We've been looking at the various fruit of contentment and how we'll react to life when contentment is absorbed into our thoughts and attitudes. Developing contentment takes time and practice, but the fruit of the Spirit that characterize a contented person are worth your commitment.

As we close, let's consider the following poem written by an unknown Confederate soldier and see whether our new attitudes of contentment are similar to his:

"I asked God for strength that I might achieve; I was made weak that I might learn humbly to obey.

"I asked God for health that I might do greater things; I was given infirmity that I might do better things.

"I asked for riches that I might be happy; I was given poverty that I might be wise.

"I asked for power that I might have the praise of men; I was given weakness that I might feel the need of God.

"I asked for all things that I might enjoy life; I was given life that I might enjoy all things.

"I got nothing that I asked for but everything I had hoped for.

"Almost despite myself, my unspoken prayers were answered and among all men I am most richly blessed."

NOTES: 1. Charles D. Kelley, "The Miracle of Contentment," *Discipleship Journal*, Issue 42 (November/December 1987), page 29.